Self-Hatred

Why Do We Hate Ourselves?
– Beyond Self-Hatred: Methods to Regain Inner Peace

MuRu

The Wisdom of Five Life Domains Contained in This
Book

This book addresses the topic of 'self-hatred' while offering
methods for healing various traumas, ways to protect
oneself from emotional wounds in daily life, insights about
human relationships, and guidance for psychological
maturity.

The MuRu Center

self-hatred

Why Do We Hate Ourselves?
- Beyond Self-Hatred: Methods to Regain Inner Peace
Author: MuRu

Published by | Lee Kyung-hee
Publishing House | The MuRu Center
Email | philosophus@naver.com
ISBN: 979-8-9922999-0-8

This book is dedicated as a product of humanity's collective consciousness and unconscious. This stands as testament to our shared creative spirit, as all works—whether in literature, art, engineering, scientific research, music, performance, or even moments of leisure—emerge from our collective endeavors. The intrinsic value of a creation remains unchanged whether it touches the mind of one person or the minds of billions. Everything that each of us creates is, in essence, a collaborative creation of our entire human species. Regardless of how great or small its usefulness or reputation may be, everything holds important value in the vast tapestry of human endeavor.

Don't try to be happy. Create 'happiness itself.'

\- MuRu

Table of Contents

Preface | One Cannot Live While Hating Oneself

Chapter 1: How Did Self-Love Transform Into Self-Hatred?

1.1　Originally I Am Superior, Therefore I Hate Myself

1.2　Their Criticism Has Somehow Become 'Mine'

1.3　Self-blame and guilt are the mind's attempt to change what cannot be changed

1.4　I Am Even Dependent on the 'Negative Self'

1.5　I preemptively defend against others' aversion toward me through self-destructive behavior

1.6　'Reality validation' as a psychological anesthetic

1.7　Wrongdoings always require a 'scapegoat'

1.8　I too am an 'other' to myself who deserves fair treatment

1.9　The magical incantation: 'Nevertheless, I choose not to be consumed by it'

Chapter 2: How Does Self-Hatred Transform into Aversion Toward Others?

2.1　Is That Person Really Worth Hating?

2.2　Projection is neither the 'Inner Shadow' nor malevolence

2.3　Admiration and jealousy stem from a sense of superiority

2.4　Absolving oneself by punishing others

2.5   Your projection has nothing to do with that external object

2.6   Let us transcend projection by gaining insight into the polarity of projection

Chapter 3: 'I' Am Not a Being Determined by Content

3.1   Identity is a feeling, not content

3.2   Will you become an existence living according to the scenario, or will you become the subject who creates the scenario?

3.3   Why do we need recognition from others and the world?

3.4   What we truly fear is not 'decision' but 'experience'

3.5   We need not rush to be 'ultimately right'

3.6   There are no bad personalities, only unskilled masters

3.7   The essence of life lies not in its content but in its utilization

3.8   The story of The Girl who suddenly discovered 'herself' one day

Chapter 4: Trauma - Not About Avoiding It But Making It Insignificant

4.1   Trauma is not something to eliminate, but to embrace and transcend

4.2   How to remain unhurt by others' words

4.3   How to become indifferent to 'that memory' that

troubles you

4.4 When bad memories surface, it's actually an opportunity for growth

4.5 How to Liberate Yourself from Negative Emotions

4.6 Methods for Overcoming the Instinctive Fear of the Unfamiliar

4.7 To What Extent Am I 'Willingly' Experiencing Myself?

Chapter 5: For Those Who Aspire to Be Protagonists in Their Relationships

5.1 A Message to Those Who Believe They Are Not Protagonists

5.2 Do Not Devalue Yourself

5.3 How to Handle 'Opposing Viewpoints' That Distress You

5.4 Cease Being a 'Pushover'

5.5 Cultivate Horizontal Love, Not Vertical Dependency

5.6 Empathy Does Not Require Becoming an Emotional Dumping Ground

5.7 Apologies: For Myself, For Others, For Everyone

5.8 Rediscovering Myself Through My Other Self

5.9 You and I are neither 'two separate entities' nor simply 'one'. We are 'Duality within unity'

5.10 Two Truths (N Truths - N Ranges from 0 to Infinity)

Conclusion | Don't Pursue Happiness. Create 'Happiness

Itself'
About The Author
Books By This Author

Preface: One Cannot Live While Hating Oneself

"By freeing yourself from the unconscious bonds of self-hatred through this book, you will discover solutions not only to your personal challenges, but also to relational difficulties and various life problems."

- It was a very unusual case

It happened long ago. Someone sought help for personal issues—specifically, psychological difficulties. The most significant concern was their 'negative self-image'. Their self-negation, self-deprecation, and self-distrust were severe. From childhood, their father's negative influence had been substantial. The father was socially successful. However, the parenting style of this father, intoxicated with his own success, functioned as poison to the child. No matter what efforts were made or what results were achieved, the child could never obtain their father's satisfaction. Even when bringing home the highest marks in competitions with others, all that awaited was the reproach: 'You think this is enough?' Fortunately, after spending considerable time together, the shattered self-esteem and self-image were eventually restored, though it was by no means an easy journey.

The 'unusual case' mentioned earlier occurred during the initial stages. One day, I emphatically explained to him that the 'negative self-image' composed of self-negation, self-deprecation, and self-distrust did not represent his true appearance nor his authentic self. We had reached the stage where concrete processing was necessary.

His reaction was quite peculiar. He appeared to be experiencing some form of discomfort. When I referenced his negative aspects, stating 'This is not your authentic self from that period,' I observed that he felt as though he were being dismissed, negated, and assaulted. Despite these being aspects he needed to process and release for his own well-being, he was paradoxically attempting to preserve them.

It was at that moment that I realized. 'Ah, people naturally consider their negative aspects as part of themselves! They depend on these aspects even while suffering from them.' In other words, I had witnessed one manifestation of the psychology of self-hatred.

◆ ◆ ◆

The theme of 'self-hatred' clearly crystallized in my mind much later. While engaging with many individuals through coaching, counseling, education, and study groups focused on human psychology and consciousness, I developed a strong conviction that many problems related to the 'self' might be fundamentally connected to this phenomenon.

When I first discussed this topic with people around me, most showed little interest or responded negatively. At that time, I had not yet fully grasped the severity of the 'self-hatred' mechanism and phenomenon. Now the situation has reversed. Most people show interest in this topic. This indicates that many people are troubled by this issue and seeking solutions.

People live with the psychology of self-hatred to varying degrees, whether significant or subtle. Sometimes it manifests as minor self-criticism or self-reflection, while at other times it takes the form of moderate self-regret. In some cases, it manifests as severe self-deprecation, aversion, sense of guilt, feelings of guilt, or despair.

These are all forms of self-hatred, differing only in intensity. In other words, it is the self harboring hatred toward itself.

Self-hatred makes life miserable. It prevents one from living life properly and enjoying what should rightfully be experienced to the fullest. Life's motivation and energy are wasted, creating difficulties for both oneself and those in one's surroundings.

In particular, Korea, a leading example of both an exhaustion-driven and competition-based society, exhibits particularly strong psychological patterns of self-hatred in both individuals and groups due to its social structure. Surprisingly, many individuals live without recognizing their own patterns of self-hatred or tendencies toward self-deprecation. This phenomenon is intrinsically connected to social structures characterized by intense competition and oppression. Furthermore, because it is such a universal experience, it often fails to be recognized as a problematic condition.

'Self-hatred' constitutes a diagnostic framework. The purpose of this book is to fundamentally investigate, understand, and provide insight into this psychological phenomenon. An additional aim is to share specific perspectives and methodologies for resolving and transcending this issue, addressing both individual and collective domains.

First, we must recognize that we are collectively and unconsciously trapped in excessive self-hatred psychology. With any problem, we must first acknowledge that 'it exists' before we can move to the next step. The next step is solving it. We cannot continue living while hating ourselves. However, we should not hastily turn away from self-hatred. Self-hatred cannot be resolved by suppressing, repressing, avoiding, or ignoring it. Such responses only deepen the problem or create adverse side effects. We need proper methods, not avoidance, suppression, or ignorance. We must establish a life attitude that neither becomes consumed by our emotions nor suppresses or avoids them—one that 'willingly embraces while simultaneously transcending.' For the happiness of ourselves and others. This book was written with that intention.

The core contents of the five chapters in this book are as follows:
-Chapter 1 < How Did Self-Love Transform Into Self-Hatred?> explores in detail the hidden psychological mechanisms and fundamental causes of 'self-hatred,' the core theme of this book. Surprisingly, we often fail to understand our own psychology. Chapter 1 examines why we come to hate ourselves and identifies the nature of our original psychological state. Through this exploration, we discover that self-hatred is not actually self-hatred, allowing us to free ourselves from its grip. We become capable of treating ourselves fairly and objectively.

The subsequent four chapters each address independent areas while ultimately contributing to the resolution of self-hatred. In other words, the content of the four chapters following Chapter 1 can be used to address the issue of 'self-hatred', but beyond that, each chapter independently contains valuable insights for resolving various psychological, relational, and everyday challenges in life.

-Chapter 2 < How Does Self-Hatred Transform into Aversion Toward Others?> addresses 'misanthropy' directed at others, specifically the concept of 'projection'. A significant portion of self-hatred originates from pathological projection and negative projection. Misanthropy is essentially the projection of self-hatred. A person who loves themselves in a healthy way never unjustly develops aversion toward others. People live within unhealthy psychological projections without recognizing them. The better you understand your psychological projection mechanisms, the more freedom you can gain from self-hatred and misanthropy.

-**Chapter 3 <'I' Am Not a Being Determined by Content>** is a discourse on 'identity'. Identity is the most crucial issue in life that concerns everyone. Society and adults should help children develop appropriate identities, yet ironically, many adults themselves lack healthy and clear identities. Through this chapter, you will comprehend the essence of identity that you have unconsciously and vaguely understood, and learn methods to develop a healthy and mature sense of identity.

-**Chapter 4 <Trauma: Not About Avoiding It But Making It Insignificant>** is a discourse on 'trauma and healing'. Self-hatred originates from emotional traumas inflicted by others and the world in our past. This chapter specifically addresses methods to heal and effectively cope with those traumas. You will learn to 'embrace and transcend' traumas without becoming obsessed with them, avoiding them, or suppressing them.

-**Chapter 5 < For Those Who Aspire to Be Protagonists in Their Relationships>** explores 'relationships and empathy'. It is fundamentally a discourse on 'human relationships'. Self-hatred is not merely an individual problem but also an issue of collective dimension. We tend to view life and the world centered on our 'individual self', but such a perspective inevitably reaches its limitations. This is because we are beings of relationship, and are completed through our connections with others. In the latter part of this chapter, I introduce new perspectives called 'unity with two polarities' and 'two truths'. We are neither two separate entities nor a uniform unity. Each pole maintains its uniqueness while harmonizing to create a new wholeness. Through this 'self-expansion,' we can ultimately transcend self-hatred.

Now, let us embark on an interesting journey of thought together. However, there is a fundamental premise. When addressing the topic of 'self-hatred,' we must not confine all related issues to merely individual problems. There exist numerous social structural, political, and economic problems that cause this condition, and sometimes these extend beyond the scope of an individual's effort, will, and capabilities. Therefore, let us not claim that everything can be resolved through individual change alone. Nor can it be solved through social change alone. Solutions must be pursued in both domains: the individual and society. The content discussed in this book is not necessarily confined to the individual domain. The principles and perspectives presented here can be readily extended to address collective phenomena and problems as well.

If there are things we can and should do for social change, let us commit to doing them to the best of our ability. This includes participation in political parties, NGOs, and social movements. It is also possible within each of the communities to which we belong. Let us do our utmost with those external actions we can take. Simultaneously, we must focus on personal, internal work using the perspective and approach I discuss in my writing.

The Wisdom of Five Life Domains Contained in This Book

- Overcoming self-hatred—a distorted form of self-love—and reclaiming self-acceptance.
- Stop the misguided hatred toward others, which is merely an external projection of self-hatred.
- Neither others nor society, but you yourself determine your own identity.
- Transform past traumas into insignificant memories without 'suppressing, distorting, or avoiding' them.
- Become the master of your relationships, not their slave.

Chapter 1: How Self-Love Transformed Into Self-Hatred

1.1   Originally I Am Superior, Therefore I Hate Myself

1.2   Their Criticism Has Somehow Become 'Mine'

1.3   Self-blame and guilt are the mind's attempt to change what cannot be changed

1.4   I Am Even Dependent on the 'Negative Self'

1.5   I preemptively defend against others' aversion toward me through self-destructive behavior

1.6   'Reality validation' as a psychological anesthetic

1.7   Wrongdoings always require a 'scapegoat'

1.8   I too am an 'other' to myself who deserves fair treatment

1.9   The magical incantation: 'Nevertheless, I choose not to be consumed by it'

1.1 Originally I Am Superior, Therefore I Hate Myself
: The Self-Love Hidden Within Self-Hatred

No one truly hates themselves at their core.

Nevertheless, everyone harbors some degree of self-hatred.

This causes considerable suffering.

How does this come to be?

The primary reason lies in the insidious nature of self-hatred. No one openly despises themselves or deliberately inflicts self-harm. On the contrary, we all profoundly love ourselves. The most powerful instincts in living organisms are the self-protective instinct and the self-preservation instinct. Despite this, nearly all of us experience the psychology of self-hatred, which progresses from weak personal boundaries to self-regret, then to self-disappointment and self-deprecation, and ultimately to profound self-hatred.

However, there is a crucial fact that we must not overlook. The underlying psychology of self-hatred is actually rooted in 'self-love' and 'self-superiority.' This applies to both its origin and development. In other words, while the outcome manifests as self-hatred, it actually represents an attempt to do something for one's own benefit. The purpose is to become 'a better self' by creating internal tension or self-admonishment through self-hatred. These mechanisms do indeed produce certain effects. However, in most cases, the positive effects are negligible while the negative consequences grow increasingly significant. Therein lies the problem.

Every person seeks to validate the legitimacy of their self-existence. Moreover, they desire to confirm their own superiority.

Isn't this true not only for humans but for all existing entities? They wish to feel and think positively about themselves. However, the reality before them often contradicts this desire. They fail to meet the standards or levels to which they aspire.

Now, consider this: whose image serves as the source of standards and levels for this comparison? It is, in fact, one's own image—the idealized version of oneself that one envisions. It is perceiving and conceptualizing oneself as exceptional and superior. Regardless of actual reality, within one's inner self, this becomes the 'truth'.

This constructed 'self' experiences disappointment, limitations, inadequacy, and imperfection when confronting the reality of who we actually are—a self that has not yet reached that idealized standard. Therefore, one instinctively attempts to compensate for and protect oneself, driven by the belief that one must not remain inferior or inadequate.

At this point, our mind devises and implements an extraordinarily subtle strategy. It involves separating the inferior and inadequate self from what is perceived as the 'real' self, then assuming the position of a superior self that objectifies and despises this inadequate version of oneself. This creates a peculiar form of self-salvation—the self is saved through the sacrifice of the self.

People rarely recognize the subtle separation and self-protective mechanisms operating within this process. Most individuals interpret these feelings merely as self-hatred, self-destructive behavior, self-loathing, or a sense of guilt. What functions as self-protection at the unconscious level manifests as self-hatred at the surface consciousness level, and this contradiction between the two domains creates profound confusion for the individual. And they continue to struggle within an ingenious self-deception that torments them without fully understanding this confusion.

Eventually, quality of life deteriorates, everyday happiness is threatened, and the validity of one's existence becomes traumatized. This strategy of establishing an inferior self and superior self, and securing 'the legitimacy of self-existence' by mistreating oneself as if mistreating others, may seem plausible initially but is ultimately destined to fail.

The first reason for failure is that neither the inadequate self nor the superior self actually exists. When we attempt to accomplish something by establishing constructs that don't exist, it may seem to work initially, but becomes increasingly difficult over time, and ultimately nothing improves. Fantasies cannot manifest reality.

The second reason for failure is that this is ultimately deception—a clever yet foolish self-deception of the mind. No matter how much we separate ourselves and claim to embody the superior self rather than the inadequate self, the mind knows all too well that these two cannot be separated. That the two are ultimately one unity.

Sometimes we experience a strange pleasure in the process of self-hatred, contempt, and aversion. Or we may develop the illusion that we have overcome and conquered something. But whether it concerns the body or the mind, even kindergarten children understand that if you hurt yourself, you alone feel the pain. Nevertheless, we continue to engage in self-hatred. Why? It is because we have failed to clearly recognize the hidden mechanisms explained earlier. It is because we have not clearly identified the misunderstood aspects, structural errors, and procedural immaturities.

To become free from the prison of self-hatred, one must clearly recognize its structure and process. Before attempting specific solutions, one must clearly recognize that the entire process of 'self-separation,' 'self-objectification,' and 'self-hatred' that one has been unconsciously engaging in was initially an attempt to establish oneself more firmly and secure a sense of superiority. It's simply not effective. This insight, this recognition, must first become clear. One must not only understand intellectually but achieve clear self-awareness.

The next step requires addressing past habits and ingrained resistance. Mere recognition does not resolve everything. Oil paint that has dried on your hands doesn't wash away in a single attempt. Complete removal requires multiple washings. A car traveling at high speed cannot immediately stop or change direction simply by applying the brakes or turning the steering wheel. One must sustain effort until the inertia dissipates completely.

Just as inertia exists in the physical world, there is also inertia in the realm of our minds. Even when we notice and realize something, we have merely begun to apply the brakes and turn the steering wheel. We now require physical time for the inertia of 'past habits or stubbornness' to be sufficiently counteracted. And this requires somewhat more attentive handling than physical inertia.

Inertia is merely inertia. Habits and stubbornness are not absolute. Even before these issues are completely resolved, there is no need to continue suffering from them. Above all, we need not perpetuate our self-hatred. This is the most crucial point. Once you recognize the subtle yet misguided structure and process of self-hatred, you have 'already' applied the brakes and changed direction. The remaining journey involves continuously recognizing that lingering feelings and tendencies are merely habits and stubbornness, and not stopping the transformation. Through awareness, you have already halted the pattern, and your course has already shifted.

Summary

No one truly hates themselves, but everyone dislikes themselves to some extent. This stems from the subtlety of self-hatred. The source of self-hatred is actually self-love and a superiority complex. Self-hatred is an attempt to transform oneself into a better existence, though ultimately its negative effects outweigh any benefits. Self-hatred emerges from the separation and objectification between the inferior and superior ego, functioning as a self-protection strategy. By clearly recognizing this mechanism, one can liberate oneself from self-hatred. For this purpose, one must address the inertia of past habits and attachments. To cease self-hatred, one must continuously transform by recognizing remaining emotions and directional tendencies as habits and attachments in real-time.

1.2 Their Criticism Has Somehow Become 'Mine'

: Separating thoughts from the 'self'

Human psychology is not a domain where, like physical objects, only a single mode, explanation, and analysis exists. Therefore, numerous alternative interpretations and analyses are entirely possible. In any case, the key consideration is how much 'practical help' can be obtained through that interpretation and analysis—in other words, its utility.

Precise and accurate insight naturally evokes practical solutions. Sometimes insight itself becomes the solution, while at other times, specific solutions emerge naturally after insight, with a time delay. Either way, both approaches are beneficial.

Previously, we examined how superiority complex gives rise to self-hatred. Now, we will explore another cause that generates self-hatred. By identifying with our own thoughts, we develop a negative self-image. To state the conclusion first: my thoughts are not me.

- Negative thoughts implanted by the external world

During childhood, information is primarily collected and absorbed from external sources. Then, as we mature, we gradually begin to generate various thoughts from within ourselves. Of course, in all cases, information from external sources and information generated internally influence each other. There is never a purely unidirectional process. However, no matter how much humans think and reflect independently, the foundation of these thoughts is information received from external sources. Let us remember this. Most of what exists within me has originated from the external world.

Let us connect this mechanism to one's self-concept or self-image. We cannot independently create our own self-image. From childhood, our self-image is formed through a combination of information provided by parents, family, others, and the world, along with our individual temperament or disposition and patterns of thought. That is, elements from the external and internal worlds combine together. Which element has a greater influence may vary slightly depending on an individual's disposition or characteristics.

Every person's self-image is formed in this manner. The problem lies in the 'negative self-image' that causes one to hate oneself. A negative self-image forms unconsciously, and one continues to be influenced by it. The negative self-image that depletes one's life energy and motivation is, if following the previously mentioned pattern, ultimately something injected from external sources. Whether by individuals or by the external environment and society. While it may occasionally be formed partly due to an innate negative or pessimistic disposition, fundamentally, external influences and internalized messages should be considered the primary factors.

The period when external messages about self-image are internalized typically occurs during childhood, and the figures who exert the greatest influence are, of course, parents. Additionally, relatives, friends, teachers, and acquaintances encountered during one's formative years also contribute incrementally to the development of one's self-image. Young children cannot actively discern which information to accept or reject, and instead absorb most of it indiscriminately. Even negative information they might wish to reject is unconsciously accepted as 'true'.

The self-image imposed from external sources often contains numerous negative elements. These primarily relate to an individual's abilities or personal attributes. Comments such as having no talents, being incompetent, or being lazy. Alternatively, they might concern one's appearance or intrinsic worth. Remarks such as being unattractive, or not being a person of value. In relatively mature societies, numerous educational and cultural mechanisms are established to minimize negative influences on children, but such protections are absent in immature societies. Adult generations who developed with a negative self-image inevitably transmit this influence to children. Consequently, an individual's self-image becomes characterized by uniformity, negativity, and repression rather than shared identity or positivity.

- Mistaking their thoughts for 'my own thoughts'

This is precisely where the problem lies. From a certain moment, we begin to mistake injected external perspectives as 'my own unique thoughts.' From this point onward, we no longer recognize that these perspectives originated externally. This even applies to content we initially rejected. While we consciously rejected it, it had unconsciously entered our minds.

In a way, 'external thoughts' and 'internal thoughts' may not be clearly distinguishable from the beginning. That is, we merely create the distinction, but regardless of internal or external origin, only 'thoughts' exist. Thus, we can easily fall into the illusion of mistaking external thoughts for our own internal ones.

Just as it is natural for our self-image to be formed by external influences, there is no significant problem in adopting externally sourced thoughts as our own unique perspectives. Rather, this can be viewed as a function that naturally evolved as humans developed complex and profound thinking abilities unique to our species through our distinctive capacity for language. It is simply a tool of unity. One must clearly distinguish and recognize the structure and process of this journey. Without this awareness, we unconsciously repeat patterns.)

The real problem emerges in the final stage.

- Identifying my thoughts with 'myself' and clinging to them stubbornly

The problems are negative thoughts, negative information, and negative self-images. Let us focus our discussion on negative self-image.

Whether imposed from external sources or generated internally, the solution is to discard, ignore, or halt negative self-images that torment us, create difficulty, and drain our energy—whenever circumstances permit. Or it would be more beneficial for me to transform them into positive, proactive elements.

We cannot simply change, discard, or ignore our negative self-image. Even when people tell me, 'You are quite attractive. You are excellent.' 'You are doing well,' I tend to deny it. Outwardly, I might say, 'Really?' 'Thank you' while nodding, but internally I do not believe it. The self that I feel, acknowledge, and accept still seems like an inadequate, incompetent, unattractive, and meaningless existence. Within our minds, the negative self-image, self-hatred, and self-negation that we have carried throughout our lives continue to operate. Even while declaring, 'I dislike this. I want to change it,' these patterns persist.

Why does this happen? As beings with inherently selfish instincts, why are we unable to make choices that benefit ourselves in this area, instead opting for choices that harm us?

It is because we fail to recognize the hidden paradox within this contradiction. In essence, this reaction occurs due to our lack of awareness. When we clearly and distinctly recognize this pattern, it naturally begins to dissolve. That contradiction is precisely the mechanism of identification between 'one's thoughts' and 'oneself.'

You think you already know about mechanisms like 'identification'? No, you don't. If you had truly noticed and recognized it clearly, you would have already changed. No matter how much you understand it intellectually, theoretically, or as accumulated knowledge, if you haven't actually recognized it, noticed it, become self-aware of it, or experienced awakening about it, you must honestly admit that you 'don't know.' You must acknowledge that you are still in a state of not knowing. If you remain under the illusion that you know when you still don't, you are depriving yourself of the opportunity to truly know. You must actually notice it. Or become self-aware of it. Therefore, automatic identification should no longer be allowed to occur. Or one must recognize identification so as not to be unconsciously swept away or buried in it. It is not about stopping or eliminating identification through some kind of effort, nor is it about ignoring or suppressing it. It naturally ceases when we notice and become aware of it.

To put it more simply, it is about no longer being 'stubborn' or becoming attached. It refers to the conscious act of identification where we equate 'my thoughts' with 'myself.' Alternatively, it means not treating my thoughts as absolute truth. When necessary, assert and utilize them strongly, but when unnecessary, learn to pass over them lightly or let them go entirely.

You ask how to handle still thinking negatively despite your efforts? You wonder if it should be easy? That's precisely why I've termed it 'stubbornness.' You're not continuing this pattern due to ignorance. Everyone knows or feels this to some extent, yet they remain reluctant to relinquish the belief or mental habit that 'my thoughts constitute who I am.' Of course, this 'reluctance to let go' can often be deeply unconscious. There may be cases where one says 'I want to let go too!' yet remains unable to do so. However, ultimately, one is choosing not to let go. This must be recognized and acknowledged.

Whether injected from external sources or arising from within, a 'thought' is merely a thought. Thoughts are not 'me'. When you identify thoughts as yourself, you fall into the error of trying to defend those thoughts, following the instinct to preserve your sense of existence.

- Just because something attracts attention does not mean it is important.

Everyone possesses an instinct to preserve their own existential identity. Physically, we strive to protect our life and safety, while mentally and psychologically, we attempt to maintain our existential integrity. For bodily existence, we diligently nourish ourselves and take actions to protect and maintain our physical form. And to sustain our mental and psychological existence, we seek recognition from both ourselves and others. These are all natural instincts and entirely normal behaviors.

The problem arises when we try to hold onto something even when there is no need to do so. That is, various forms of suffering and problems emerge when we strive to maintain things that are essentially unrelated to preserving and sustaining our physical or mental existentiality. One of these is the negative thoughts we have already acquired, especially our negative self-image.

Negative thoughts or a negative self-image may serve their own purposes. Humans have evolved to pay more attention to and assign greater importance to negative things rather than positive ones. Positive things cause no harm even when we don't deliberately attend to or nurture them, so we can leave them unattended. In essence, we tend to ignore them. This is also a matter of efficiency.

Negative things, however, should not be left unattended. This is because we cannot predict when they might harm us, cause suffering, or create problems. They are unpredictable threats. Therefore, our consciousness and attention must focus on the negative. Only then can we protect ourselves. This represents a fundamental self-protective instinct.

Problems arise when we mistakenly equate 'what captures our attention' with 'what is important.' Or we misinterpret it as 'that is factual and more correct.' We are merely allocating more attention as needed, but we erroneously conclude it is 'because that thing is important, factual, and correct.'

To this is added the consciousness pattern of self-assurance that 'I am right.' We humans fundamentally operate with the underlying psychological assumption that 'I am right.' This is not incorrect. It is akin to an animal instinct of unity. Every existence needs an instinctive feeling in their inner self that 'What I am doing is right. I am doing well' in order to function properly and engage in activities. Without this, one would always be restless and flustered. Therefore, the self-assurance that we automatically possess is entirely natural.

The problem arises when the feeling 'I am right. I am correct' is applied uniformly. Even when objectively I could be wrong or need to make corrections, I still maintain 'I am right. Becoming entrenched in the feeling that 'I am right' and stubbornly clinging to it will ultimately cause harm to myself.

◆ ◆ ◆

When the three mechanisms I have explained thus far combine, the final error becomes extremely powerful. That is, there is an identification between 'my thoughts' and 'myself,' compounded by the illusion that 'negative thoughts and negative self-image are factual, significant, and correct.' And finally, it connects to the belief 'I am right' and 'I am protecting myself.' Through the incorrect use of the instinct to 'maintain myself,' and the belief that 'I am right.' It is through the misapplication of the instinct that 'I am right' that we cling to a negative self-image and self-hatred. Even though it actually harms our authentic self. A tragic misconception.

What should we do? If the mechanisms of self-negation and self-hatred that torment us are so unconscious and seemingly inevitable, must we helplessly continue to hate and negate ourselves?

Absolutely not. There is certainly a way. First, let us become more clearly aware of the hidden mechanisms of self-hatred that I mentioned earlier. It's about noticing and recognizing these patterns. This isn't just intellectual understanding or theoretical knowledge, but maintaining clear awareness in our daily lives.

Next, we need to create a 'process of bringing the Unconscious into consciousness.' Until now, when the mechanisms and reactions described earlier occurred, they happened unconsciously, and we, as the individuals involved, repeated them unconsciously and automatically. Now, when these processes occur, we must consciously observe them. This is the practice of self-awareness and recognition. It is actively and proactively raising consciousness by saying, 'Ah, this is what this means.' Without consciousness-raising, we essentially remain in ignorance. Whereas previously we might have assumed that our actions and experiences were naturally correct and beneficial, now we must examine and discern them with critical detachment. We must determine whether something is truly appropriate and beneficial for us, or merely harmful patterns repeated through unconscious instinct and habit.

One must recognize that it is 'a thought injected from outside' rather than 'my own unique thought.' The same applies to one's self-image. We must recognize that a significant portion of our self-image may have been injected from external sources. This is not suggesting that you should deny or consider your entire current self-image as incorrect, but rather that you need to identify which specific parts of it are externally imposed. We must recognize that we have mistakenly identified these external impositions as our own unique self-image.

Finally, we must stop equating 'my thoughts' with 'myself.' Thoughts are merely thoughts, not my identity. Stopping, denying, or modifying thoughts is not an action performed upon 'myself.' Feeling negated as a person simply because someone disagrees with my thoughts is purely my own illusion.

We must cease unconsciously treating negative thoughts as 'factual and significant,' and also stop the indiscriminate application of the belief that 'I am right. I am correct.' The goal isn't to suppress or ignore these thoughts, but rather to notice them. The more clearly we develop self-awareness, the more naturally these patterns will cease. It's about relinquishing unnecessary mental stubbornness, rigid adherence, and attachments that appear reasonable but actually cause us harm. We do this for our own well-being.

When necessary, you should certainly hold firm to your own thoughts, and strongly communicate and realize your assertions to others and the world. The same applies to your self-image. Make it clear and show it to others and the world. That is fundamental and entirely natural. The key is recognizing when there is no need to do so. When there is no particular need to assert yourself, you can simply make the most appropriate choice according to the situation.

It's quite simple. And acting this way is truly in your self-interest.

Because it is most beneficial to your own well-being.

Instead of behaving ambivalently selfish, let us endeavor to become genuinely selfish. Rather than passively following habitual patterns and incurring losses, let us consciously and deliberately regulate the flow of our thoughts and reactions to maximize our personal benefit.

◆ ◆ ◆

Summary

Self-hatred originates when we mistake externally imposed negative thoughts as our own and identify these thoughts with our ego. We must separate thoughts from the ego, recognize the origins of negative thinking, and bring unconscious processes into consciousness. One must realize that thoughts are simply thoughts, not one's true self. By doing so, one can release unnecessary attachments and make choices that are truly beneficial to oneself.

1.3 Self-blame and guilt are the mind's attempt to change what cannot be changed

: Self-blame and guilt are forms of selfishness

The third hidden psychological aspect of self-hatred that we will examine together is the sense of guilt and feelings of guilt.

The sense of guilt and feelings of guilt are somewhat evident psychological phenomena. While the previously mentioned 'distortion of self-love' and 'identification with negative thoughts' are mechanisms that occur unconsciously, the sense of guilt and feelings of guilt are expressions of self-hatred that everyone engages in with full awareness.

There are hidden mechanisms at work here as well. The more clearly you become self-aware of this, the closer you come to freeing yourself from self-hatred.

- Accepting the past and present reality with confidence and dignity

The true nature of guilt and sense of guilt is objective self-reflection and self-examination. This too poses no significant problem when not taken to excess. However, by becoming excessively conscious of one's mistakes, errors, incompetence, failures, and inadequacies, what should be healthy self-reflection often transforms into self-blame, self-destructive behavior, and guilt that torments the self.

All forms of 'self-blame' that extend beyond feedback, reflection, and contemplation about past events are unnecessary and sometimes burden not only ourselves but also those around us. Furthermore, it depletes our energy when we need to objectively assess situations and develop appropriate solutions, causing us to collapse and accomplish nothing. There are several reasons why people become trapped in unnecessary and impractical psychological patterns of self-blame, unable to transcend them.

Regarding negative situations they have caused or are connected to, people generally consciously or unconsciously add thoughts such as 'my fault, my responsibility, my incompetence.' 'This happened because I did something wrong.' It is the feeling and thought that 'this happened because I am incompetent.' However, in reality, there is no such thing as 'completely my fault.' Of course, I bear some responsibility, but in the same situation, there is a high probability that similar results would have occurred even if it were someone else. Nevertheless, because the person who failed or made the mistake is none other than 'me,' we feel a sense of responsibility. Problems arise when this becomes excessive and leads to self-blame. Even when others say it's okay, one doesn't stop blaming oneself. Why is that?

It is because we dream 'different dreams' as a result of not accepting our past and our past selves. We stubbornly refuse to accept reality that has already occurred, wishing instead for 'a different self, different results, different circumstances.' But these remain merely wishes, unable to change our past and present reality. Different dreams and different wishes may appear to benefit us at first glance, but in reality, we are merely deceiving ourselves. This happens to everyone at times in life. We make choices believing they will benefit us, only to find they ultimately cause us suffering. The sense of guilt and guilt itself operate precisely in this manner.

The only and wisest response is 'complete acceptance.' Let's not misunderstand this. The 'acceptance' mentioned here is not about giving up, despairing, or helplessly submitting. On the contrary, it means embracing the past and reality that already exist with the most active and proactive mindset, with dignity and confidence. It means permitting that existence, with oneself as the true subject of life and being. Expressed differently, it could also be called 'willingly experiencing' or 'willingly undergoing.' It's not because they are good, well-executed, or justified. It's simply allowing them because they already existed.

Whether I permit it or not, the past no longer exists. Nevertheless, because we dream of different circumstances, we cannot accept the existence of the past and continuously attempt to deny it. Despite its impossibility, we persistently deny it while believing it possible. The denied past may include others and situations, but ultimately, the central element is 'myself'. When we cannot accept and acknowledge our past self, self-negation inevitably occurs, giving rise to self-blame and guilt. Despite the pain and difficulty, we desperately want to eliminate our past self, our insufficient self— the version of ourselves we wish not to be.

While these efforts and struggles are commendable and entirely understandable, they regrettably constitute a strategy that simply does not work. Only the person struggling becomes exhausted, with no beneficial outcome. This is because such is the fundamental nature of self-blame and guilt.

- Self-blame and guilt are quite selfish

Self-blame and guilt are neither humility nor self-reflection. On the contrary, they are strategies for unconscious psychological superiority or stability and satisfaction. It is a flawed strategy, and eventually you yourself become the victim.

This might be difficult to comprehend at first glance. Why is it selfish when it involves self-awareness and taking responsibility for one's own mistakes rather than blaming others or circumstances? Of course, genuine self-reflection can indeed be constructive. However, most of our sense of guilt and feelings of guilt are created through the addition of subtle, selfish psychological mechanisms. This is why we dream of becoming a 'different version of ourselves.' It is a form of self-betrayal and self-deception. First, we set high standards and derive self-satisfaction from them. 'I am a person of this caliber. This is the kind of existence I embody. Even though in reality, I am not.'

This is also a psychological coping strategy. Because we cannot accept our current selves as they are, we create a false self and adopt it as our true identity. However, both versions are erroneous. In other words, neither the 'inadequate current self' that one perceives nor the 'excellent self' that one aspires to be is actually real.

When one's 'current self' falls short of self-imposed standards in certain situations or tasks, they experience excessive self-blame and guilt. This is described as 'selfish' precisely because it serves as an impractical superiority complex or psychological defense mechanism. Even if one has failed in reality, they desire to savor psychological superiority, satisfaction, and reassurance by envisioning an inner self that hasn't failed, isn't inadequate, but rather is impressive, capable, and successful. In doing so, a separation occurs between the real self and the actual situation. Furthermore, one becomes unable to properly perceive one's authentic self and reality, failing to conceive or implement practical responses and solutions. Ultimately, this is detrimental to oneself. Failed selfishness that harms oneself—this is the true nature of self-blame and guilt.

Does this mean we shouldn't aspire to become different? Isn't it natural for every human being to strive for self-improvement? Isn't that necessary for personal development? Indeed. If approached properly, that is correct. The purpose of this text is to properly engage in this process together.

It simply means that we need not harbor 'illusions'. The 'different appearance' mentioned here is a form of illusion. High standards and an elevated self-image that bear no relation to reality may appear impressive but are merely illusions. Illusions, in every instance, produce adverse effects rather than benefits. Therefore, instead of illusions, let us establish thoroughly realistic and practical goals and strategies, and evaluate whether they truly benefit us. This means modifying strategies that are impractical and harmful. For myself, not for anyone else.

Illusions are often injected by others and the world rather than created by ourselves. Rather than from healthy and rational judgment, we passively and unconsciously accept external images, and then mistake them for 'the self-image we desire.' Various adverse effects arise from this misconception. For example, regardless of gender, desiring what society deems desirable—an attractive physique, beautiful face, or tall stature—falls into this category. It also includes developing what might be called a 'superior mental fortitude.' This encompasses finding a socially recognized successful partner, acquiring enviable skills and an admirable profession, and attaining knowledge, honor, and recognition. Or it might involve demonstrating one's capabilities within a community or organization to which one belongs.

As mentioned previously, if you wish to achieve something, you simply need to dedicate your best efforts toward that achievement. The crucial question is whether this is a goal I have genuinely chosen for myself or something I blindly desire because it was implanted in my consciousness. The former brings me happiness both through the process of achievement and in its results. The latter, conversely, can cause me to struggle at every moment.

We need 'our own goals' that we establish ourselves, not 'others' goals' that we mistakenly believe are our own. By doing so, we can free ourselves from the unnecessary self-blame and guilt that arise from clinging to illusions.

- The healthy prototype of self-blame and guilt is the self-protective instinct

There is an interesting story circulating in the archaeological community. It is said that in a certain region, there existed a vast swamp where countless animals had fallen to their deaths since ancient times. In the modern era, this swamp dried up and solidified into firm ground. When archaeologists excavated the area, they discovered an abundance of animal fossils that had been buried for centuries. However, there was one species notably absent from these findings—humans.

Humans, upon witnessing other animals perish in this treacherous terrain, would have recognized the danger and avoided it. Or perhaps several people may have fallen in and been rescued. Through various experiences, humans would have identified the dangers of that place and learned to avoid it. In contrast, animals lack such cognitive abilities, which is why they repeatedly fall into the same trap.

The feeling that 'something is wrong' protects us from potential future dangers. Our sense of guilt and feelings of guilt are also forms of protective instinct that shield us from potential dangers. Thus, we strive not to repeat the same mistakes or situations in the future. As if all other animals manage to avoid the swamplands that ensnare everyone else. For humans, this applies not only to physical places or obstacles but also to dangerous situations and, furthermore, to avoiding our own mistakes. In this manner, unnecessary emotional reactions eventually either supplement or completely replace the purpose of objective and neutral self-examination and self-reflection.

Even if we feel that 'something is wrong' with ourselves, and it actually is, what we should recall in that moment is not a sense of guilt but rather that we are 'wise humans who have avoided the swampland.' The 'negative feelings' we experience are merely 'useful caution' warning us not to fall into that swampland again. We simply need to acknowledge that signal and prepare well for what comes next. We can stop what needs stopping, change what requires changing, and add what should be added as we move forward.

- The problem is not self-blame or guilt, but direction

The past cannot be changed, no matter how much we 'dream differently.' This is a fact everyone knows. Continuously dreaming of and wishing for 'a changed past' is merely psychological stubbornness. In a way, it is like throwing a tantrum. I suspect that the prototype of this stubbornness might originate from our infancy, when caregivers would respond to our tantrums born out of necessity.

Once we reach a certain age, that method no longer works. Some people may continue to throw tantrums for longer periods, but for most, such reactions cease after a certain developmental stage. Beyond this point, we begin to adopt the wisest and most appropriate measures, attitudes, behaviors, and thoughts in accordance with our circumstances and reality. Everyone strives to live this way, doing their best. Traces of our infancy and early childhood may well remain within our unconscious. This occurs because we cannot permit, accept, or stop rejecting 'past incorrect situations and our past flawed selves' that have already transpired. It is essentially throwing a 'tantrum' without a specific target.

The work we must undertake is the 'conscious integration of the unconscious.' Due to the various causes mentioned earlier, an unconscious psychological tendency arises within us that seeks to deny 'the past that already exists.' We repeatedly cling to and cannot abandon this mechanism, despite its lack of utility or practical value. Merely for psychological satisfaction, comfort, and reassurance.

We must become aware that this process is occurring unconsciously. We need to notice and recognize it. The more clearly we bring these patterns into consciousness, the more our unconscious patterns and habits will gradually disappear, just as darkness naturally vanishes in the presence of light. Of course, adding conscious effort enhances this process. As this happens, our consciousness gains strength, and we will cease the regret and self-negation that unnecessarily waste our energy. With the power of consciousness developed in this manner, we will make ourselves and our surroundings healthier, and continue to fulfill our present and future potential.

Isn't this something worth trying willingly?

Summary

Self-blame and guilt originate from an unrealistic desire to alter the past. This represents a distorted form of the self-protective instinct, which is, in reality, a selfish psychological strategy. To overcome this, one must accept the past and reality as they are, and bring unconscious processes into consciousness. Rather than engaging in self-blame, it is important to learn from experiences and prepare for the future. By focusing on the present and future, one can cease unnecessary self-negation and live a healthier life.

1.4 I Am Even Dependent on the 'Negative Self'
: Existence requires no dependency

The psychological mechanism of 'self-hatred' is rather complex. In particular, it often remains hidden beyond one's conscious awareness. One such mechanism is 'dependency on the negative self.' This might sound somewhat counterintuitive. 'I depend on my negative self? That's absurd.' You might think, 'But isn't that what makes it difficult?' In reality, you are dependent on it. Through this text, let us recognize the other hidden psychological aspects of self-hatred that we unconsciously harbor, embrace them, and ultimately transcend them.

- As long as dependency exists, anxiety is inevitable

We generally believe that we dislike negative elements, distance ourselves from them, and attempt to eliminate them. In many respects, this is true. 'The negative self'—that is, the negative self-image, negative sense of self, negative sense of existence, negative self-esteem, and so forth—actually operates in the opposite manner. Unconsciously, we become dependent on it.

Are you still puzzled? 'I really want to eliminate and fix my negative self, so why do they claim that I depend on it?' you might wonder.

Consider something you truly despise. What do you typically do? Humans genuinely discard what they detest. They distance themselves from it or ignore it entirely. Yet with the 'negative self,' you cannot do this. Even when others attempt to intervene, you persistently return to your negative self, focus on it, and become captivated by it.

There is something crucial we must recognize here. Whether it is the 'positive self' or the 'negative self' is not important. The core of this mechanism is 'dependency.' Regardless of whether it is positive or negative, the very fact that I depend on something constitutes the essence. We must clearly recognize this.

Human beings depend on various external entities. These dependencies might be material possessions, relationships with others, religion, specific value systems or philosophical frameworks, achievements, physical appearance, parents, or children—virtually anything can become an object of dependency. Why do we form such dependencies? To validate our own existentiality by ourselves. It is the belief that one's existentiality is secured and validated in proportion to the value or meaning of the object upon which one depends. Naturally, the greater the value or meaning of the object, the greater my sense of existentiality becomes.

There is something we tend to overlook. The fact that we do not necessarily depend solely on positive or beneficial elements. Negative elements and harmful things can equally serve as objects of dependency for securing our existentiality, whether consciously or unconsciously. The key factor is not positivity but rather 'how dependable something is.' The greater its intensity or influence, the higher our dependency becomes.

Occasionally, individuals with mental disorders commit crimes or acts that provoke aversion in others. Through these actions, they derive satisfaction when the world and people pay attention to them, fear them, or become angry with them—because it confirms their existence. Don't we observe similar phenomena in certain online communities? In films and other media, such characters are often portrayed as serial killers.

In the psychology of self-hatred, the object of dependency becomes the 'negative self'. Though clearly negative and detrimental, we unknowingly construct this as the foundation of our existentiality or identity. Despite disliking it and suffering from it, we remain dependent upon it. If you believe you have strong tendencies toward self-negation and self-hatred, try to stop or eliminate these patterns. Make a deliberate effort to cease self-blame and despair. However, this will not be easy. This is because there are legitimate and valid reasons behind why I have come to feel this way. Regardless of whether it's good or bad, one considers viewing oneself negatively as somewhat valid.

One is merely deceiving oneself. While one might consider it healthy self-reflection or self-judgment, one is merely depending on the 'negative self' as an object for one's sense of existence and identity. Even if one has succeeded in securing existentiality through such means, the mind suffers greatly. This has negative effects on both relationships with others and daily functioning. Even that suffering ultimately becomes an object of existential dependency. It is truly a peculiar mechanism.

When friends or acquaintances tell such a person, 'You are a good person. You can do it. I can see your strengths.' 'Your worried appearance is not your true self,' nine out of ten of these individuals reject such encouragement. As mentioned earlier, it is identifying the 'negative self' as the real self.

Why do people resist attempts to break or modify their negative self-image, and instead cling to beliefs that harm them? It is because they are already dependent on these beliefs. We believe this is more valid, and it feels more familiar. This is what constitutes our 'self'.

How should we address the issue of dependency?

In many cases, the opposite—the 'positive self'—is emphasized instead. We are told to cultivate positivity and establish a new positive self-image. Of course, basing one's sense of existence and identity on the positive self rather than the negative self is a beneficial approach. Therefore, if possible, we should maximize this practice. However, it does not constitute a fundamental solution. This is because 'depending' on any object functions in the same way, as mentioned earlier. As long as we depend on something for our existentiality, value, and significance, we inevitably experience anxiety. And over time, that dependency becomes unstable and will eventually manifest in negative ways.

Why? Because my existentiality is not dependent on any internal or external object. Because my existentiality is inherently unique, meaningful, and valuable in itself.

What happens when I make my existentiality dependent on what I do well, what I achieve, how hard I work, or the recognition I receive from myself and others? If the object of dependency wavers or collapses, my existentiality wavers along with it. Even in moments when I am performing well and satisfied with recognition from both myself and others, I cannot prevent an inexplicable anxiety from casting its shadow within me. In reality, don't we fear that things might go wrong in the future even when we are thriving? This is not merely anxiety about a potential future downfall. Because I am basing my existentiality on an object that cannot be truly depended upon, anxiety naturally emerges from the depths of my inner self. Even if that object is our successful, positive self.

- That which truly exists requires no dependency

'Dependency' itself is not inherently problematic. To establish ourselves properly, leaning on or depending on something useful can be a beneficial approach. However, we must recognize that the mechanism of dependency is not absolute. It is merely a useful tool and means. In our daily lives, we 'willingly' depend on many things—not just for our identity or sense of existence. It can be either a physical tool or an abstract means. However, even if we depend on them, we should not allow our identity and existentiality to be determined by them.

The same applies to the 'negative self'. If you cannot escape from persistent self-hatred or severely suffer from self-hatred, self-deprecation, sense of guilt, or guilt, you must now clearly recognize this pattern. That it is not objective self-reflection or self-judgment, but rather that you are basing your existentiality and identity on the 'negative self'. One must recognize and acknowledge the unnecessary and futile nature of such conscious behaviors.

We must break the fragile assumption that 'without objects of dependency, my existentiality will collapse or disappear.' Similarly, we must reject the notion that 'the value and meaning of my existence are determined by the value and meaning of what I depend upon.' Though seemingly plausible, this is not truth but merely a mental construct.

My existence requires no dependency whatsoever.

My existentiality remains unique, dignified, and complete regardless of any external dependencies. The value and meaning of my existence and existentiality are not determined by the value and meaning of the dependency objects I utilize.

Let us become self-aware that there is no necessity to depend on the negative self for one's existentiality and identity. Let us recognize that this represents our instincts for self-survival, self-maintenance, and self-protection. However, we must acknowledge that we are misusing these instincts. Depending on the negative self for my existentiality offers absolutely no practical benefit. Let us clearly understand that we engage in this behavior merely because it is familiar, and because of the influences and learned patterns acquired from parents and friends.

Let us endeavor to base our existentiality and identity on the 'positive self' instead. While this transformation may not occur instantaneously, it is by no means an insurmountable challenge. Was it not I who chose to depend on the negative self in the first place? Now, I simply need to change that 'object' of dependency. Change becomes possible when we identify the necessary efforts, training, and methods, and diligently practice them.

Let us advance one step further. Let us develop the self-awareness that our existentiality and identity need not depend on either the positive or negative self. Utilize dependency as a tool, but whenever possible, lean on your positive self rather than your negative self, while always remaining aware that dependency on your positive self should not be absolute either. Always recognize that your existentiality and identity are unique, dignified, and whole, regardless of what they depend upon.

◆ ◆ ◆

Summary

One of the hidden mechanisms of self-hatred is dependence on the 'negative ego.' People often rely on their negative self to confirm their sense of existence. This causes anxiety and suffering, yet it feels familiar and safe. The solution is not transitioning to a positive ego, but recognizing that one's existence is inherently unique and valuable without dependency on any external object. Dependency should be utilized merely as a tool, and one must realize that their sense of existence is not contingent upon any external object.

1.5 Preemptively defending against others' aversion through self-destructive behavior

: Misunderstanding Self-Hatred as a Defense Strategy

Though rare, self-hatred can sometimes be mobilized as a shield against external aversion or criticism. It is to preemptively defend against the potential aversion and hatred that might come from others.

How does self-destructive behavior preemptively defend against others' aversion? There is a kind of psychological strategic error at work here. That is, believing something provides defense when it actually doesn't, or hoping that it will function in that way.

Let's examine this step by step. When we have done something wrong, what would be the appropriate action to take? First, acknowledging the mistake and engaging in self-reflection, or apologizing to the other person, or seeking forgiveness. For example, let's consider a situation where a child has done something wrong and the parents discover it. If the child confesses the wrongdoing first and asks for forgiveness, in most cases, the parents will admire the child's honesty, offer a gentle admonishment, and grant forgiveness.

In the psychology of self-hatred, this same mechanism sometimes manifests. That is, I perceive myself as somehow inadequate, deficient, and unsatisfactory. I believe others are aware of these shortcomings or will eventually discover them (this is often an excessive worry). I cannot bear their negative reactions. I cannot permit such situations to occur in the first place. So I reprimand myself before they notice. It is similar to a child acknowledging their mistake and showing contrition before being confronted. Of course, in self-hatred, this process occurs predominantly in the unconscious.

The problem is, like other mechanisms of self-hatred, this too is an 'ineffective strategy.' The part of me that engages in this behavior hopes for effectiveness, but in reality, it achieves nothing. Indeed, those who clearly understand the ineffectiveness of such methods would not engage in preemptive self-deprecation in the first place. However, as long as one unconsciously believes in its effectiveness, this pattern will automatically repeat itself despite the suffering it causes.

There is another mechanism through which preemptive self-deprecation operates. It can be described as a form of 'self-discipline,' where one hates oneself before others have a chance to dislike or hate you, thereby preemptively 'training' oneself (of course, this 'training' is a strangely distorted illusion with unconscious dimensions). Thus, even if others eventually come to hate me, the impact is diminished because I already harbor hatred toward myself. In colloquial terms, one might describe it as 'a body already abandoned, a body already surrendered.' Since I already hate myself, contempt from others becomes either inevitable or inconsequential. It's as if to say, 'I already anticipated your reaction.'

This phenomenon occurs because I objectify myself. Essentially, I become an other to myself. Self-objectification, in itself, is not inherently problematic. In fact, the more skillfully and healthily we utilize this, the more beneficial it becomes for both ourselves and others. However, preemptive self-deprecation is a form of objectification that 'mistreats' the self. It means treating ourselves poorly in the same way we might mistreat others.

This, too, is a flawed strategy. The anticipation that others will hate us is often merely an illusion. Or it could be a delusion arising from past psychological trauma. Hating myself preemptively based on this premise essentially becomes 'an illusion created in defense against another illusion.' Furthermore, preemptively hating myself has no practical preventive effect. That is to say, it has no influence on others' negative feelings toward me. Rather, it only intensifies the aversion or hatred directed toward me. No one will regard favorably a person who cannot even find worth in themselves.

◆ ◆ ◆

Summary

Self-hatred is sometimes employed as a defense mechanism against others' hostility or criticism. This manifests as an attempt to preemptively neutralize others' negative reactions or as a form of self-discipline. However, this strategy proves ineffective. In most cases, the anticipation of others' hatred is merely a delusion or the result of past psychological trauma. Self-hatred does not actually prevent others' hatred or criticism; rather, it can amplify it.

1.6 'Reality validation' as a psychological anesthetic
: Temporary and superficial psychological comfort vs. substantial and useful change

The sixth hidden psychology of self-hatred, 'reality validation,' is a concept I developed by applying the existing theory of 'system justification' to individuals. 'System justification' is a concept that requires some explanation. It is a theory established through a series of studies conducted by American political psychologist John Jost and his research team. Related content is introduced in 'Originals' written by Adam Grant, which can be summarized as follows.

In his research, the tendency to accept economic inequality was found to be higher among relatively impoverished African Americans than among European Americans. It is also reported that people belonging to the lowest income bracket were much more likely to view economic inequality as inevitable compared to those in the highest income bracket. The number of respondents willing to surrender press freedom was also twice as high. Socially vulnerable groups were more supportive of the social status quo that disadvantaged them. The research team concluded the following. "The paradoxical finding was that those who suffer the most under given conditions are the least likely to question, reject, or attempt to change them."

Through this phenomenon, Jost and his research team established what became known as 'system justification theory'. The core concept is that 'people are motivated to rationalize the status quo as legitimate'. Such rationalization occurs even when it contradicts the interests of the individual or their group.

This is because self-justification of the existing system has the effect of alleviating psychological distress. It serves as an emotional and psychological painkiller. Harboring discontent is futile and only makes one's situation more difficult. But when this happens, we lose the righteous anger to fight against injustice and are deprived of the creative will to change the world.

'System justification' is, in essence, a kind of defensive psychological mechanism that individuals develop toward society. Looking at the final section of the summary, we see the expression 'emotional and psychological painkillers.' This represents the core concept. The more socially disadvantaged individuals are, the more they become victims of the prevailing social system and structures; therefore, changing these systems would ultimately benefit them. But I believe that creating change is not easy. So instead, one voluntarily accepts that 'the world is justified exactly as it is now.' By doing so, one obtains immediate psychological comfort and alleviates suffering. From a certain perspective, this is an extremely practical coping mechanism. Even though reality doesn't improve at all and the suffering actually intensifies. That's why we use the term 'painkiller.'

It's similar to the well-known Aesop's fable, 'The Fox and the Grapes.' A fox discovers grapes hanging high above, jumps repeatedly to reach them, but ultimately fails to obtain them. As the fox departs, it remarks, 'Those grapes must be sour and inedible anyway.'

How does this connect to the psychology of self-hatred? In self-hatred, the 'system' becomes oneself and the reality and circumstances to which one belongs. In reality, one may not actually be inadequate, anxious, or dissatisfied, yet one perceives oneself in precisely these terms.

If you truly feel inadequate in some aspect of yourself, the solution is to gradually fill that void. This is the wisest, healthiest, and most appropriate response. Human feelings and emotions do not inherently contain concepts like 'deficiency' or 'dissatisfaction'. There exists only dry, objective 'measurement'. When you experience thirst, it is merely a measurement that 'the body lacks hydration,' so you drink water. When you feel cold, it is simply a measurement that 'body temperature is low,' so you warm yourself.

Whatever is measured can be filled or changed accordingly. That is the original function and purpose of measurement. This is similar to how socially disadvantaged people actively join political parties to support and vote for parties and politicians who will work on their behalf, or engage in other social movements to improve their situation.

In self-hatred, 'personal system justification' occurs. It is 'reality validation.' In other words, change is difficult to achieve, and yet leaving oneself in that state is painful, so one concludes: 'This insufficient, unsatisfactory condition is my natural state.' It is anesthetizing oneself with the self-rationalization that 'it is natural and justified.' As a result, one develops the illusion that the psychological pain has been alleviated.

Just as those who engage in system justification consider existing unequal and unreasonable social structures to be legitimate, one considers their perceived inadequacies and insufficiencies to be natural. This process ultimately reinforces self-hatred. The mind may become temporarily more comfortable, but this is never a true solution. One loses the mental strength necessary to create a healthy life and initiate personal transformation.

We must stop the flawed process. The inadequate self, the insufficient self is not who I truly am, but even if I feel that way, it is never 'something that must be accepted as is'. It is merely a 'measurement,' and we can decide what actions to take based on that measurement.

We must choose whether to seek superficial or temporary psychological comfort, or conversely, to create real, useful, and genuine change. Simply choosing not to accept such false comfort is enough. By taking just this step, we will naturally progress toward creating genuine change.

By gaining insight into and recognizing the various psychological dimensions hidden within self-hatred, we can liberate ourselves from its grip. We can end its influence. Thus, we can cease the erroneous pattern of unnecessarily hating ourselves or viewing ourselves as inadequate or insufficient. And the innate strength that resides within our inner self emerges, and with this strength as our foundation, our lives transform organically. You will live a confident and wonderful life as your authentic self, just as you are.

◆ ◆ ◆

Summary

'Reality validation' is a form of self-hatred, a psychological defense mechanism where individuals justify their inadequacies or unsatisfactory conditions. This provides temporary psychological comfort but prevents actual change. This is similar to 'system justification,' where socially disadvantaged groups justify unfair systems. The true solution is to reject such false comfort and create substantial, meaningful changes through objective assessment. Through this process, we can liberate ourselves from unnecessary self-hatred and reclaim our inherent dignity and value.

1.7 Wrongdoings always require a 'scapegoat'

: The Compulsion of the Left Hemisphere – Why the Left Hemisphere Continuously Seeks 'False Reasons'

When events occur, humans habitually identify incorrect causes or reasons rather than seeking the 'true reason.' This compulsion is unconscious rather than conscious, making it difficult for us to recognize.

The problem is that we too frequently attribute the cause of negative events to 'my fault.' Of course, we don't always blame ourselves. Sometimes we blame others or environmental factors. We may even resent fate itself. Nevertheless, because our primary concern is usually 'ourselves,' we tend to find the causes and reasons for mistakes within 'me.' This is habitual behavior. Sense of guilt and feelings of guilt arise unconsciously, making them more difficult to address properly.

Unnecessary self-blame only intensifies self-hatred and self-negation. It also hinders accurate self-reflection and insight. This is precisely what we should avoid. Simply saying 'let's not do it' doesn't automatically make it stop. This is because the root cause remains unchanged.

Neuroscience identifies 'left hemisphere obsession' as the fundamental cause of self-blame. The left hemisphere's instinctive 'need for reason fulfillment,' which compels us to create explanations in order to feel at ease, results in the adverse effect of self-negation.

The British BBC2 broadcast a six-part documentary series 'Brain Story' during July and August 2000. The following account describes an experiment featured in the sixth episode, 'The Final Mystery.' (You can find related stories by searching for 'the left hemisphere's lie' on the internet.)

In the latter part of the video, there is a story about a person named 'Joe' whose corpus callosum, which connects the right and left hemispheres of the brain, was severed through surgery. This procedure is no longer performed today, but at one time, severing the corpus callosum was used as a treatment for conditions such as epilepsy, reportedly to prevent seizures originating in one hemisphere from spreading to the other.

In that scene, they conducted a simple experiment with Joe. They show Joe a word in his right eye and ask him to identify what it is. Information entering through the right eye is transmitted to the left hemisphere, which is responsible for language, and because the left hemisphere contains language processing areas, Joe correctly identifies each word as soon as he sees it. However, when they show a word to his left eye, Joe is unable to respond. Information through the left eye goes to the right brain, but because the corpus callosum is severed, information cannot be transferred from the right brain to the left hemisphere, preventing him from linguistically reinterpreting what he has seen. Instead, when Joe was asked to draw the word he saw as a picture, he drew it accurately. Although the left hemisphere could not interpret it linguistically, the right brain had non-verbally perceived what was seen.

The key to the experiment is in the next scene: when Joe is asked, "Why did you draw that picture?" he provides his own plausible justification. For example, after seeing the word 'house' with his left eye, Joe draws a picture of a house, and when asked why he drew it, he responds with something like, "Because I've been looking for a house to move into recently." In this case, the honest and accurate answer is 'I just drew it' or 'I don't know.' Nevertheless, Joe's left hemisphere is compulsively creating reasons for this behavior.

It is said that all patients with a severed corpus callosum exhibit similar reactions. That is, visual information entering through the left eye remains in the right brain (a state where the object is non-verbally perceived but not linguistically recognized) and the person 'draws what the right brain saw.' One should answer 'I don't know' when asked about the reason for drawing that picture, but the left hemisphere, which knows nothing, steps forward and fabricates a 'false reason' as an answer. This is where the term 'the left hemisphere's lie' originated.

Our brain (especially the left hemisphere) has an obsessive need to find a specific basis, reason, or cause whenever it performs an action or makes a choice.

Let us draw inferences based on the experiment described above. It is possible that what our left hemisphere identifies is not the actual cause or reason. This is because the mechanism of the left hemisphere is not to 'tell the real reason' but rather to 'create the most plausible answer.'

One of these is unnecessary self-blame and guilt. Even if I have made mistakes and committed wrongdoings, there are numerous environmental factors beyond my control, invisible causes, and irresistible currents at play. Our brain may fail to recognize such elements, similar to how the left hemisphere cannot perceive 'something' seen by the right brain when the corpus callosum is severed. We should simply acknowledge 'I don't know' or 'just because,' but instead we fabricate plausible yet incorrect reasons (generating a sense of guilt and self-blame) and then proceed to believe in them. This represents a form of unconscious habit, stubbornness, and automatic reaction.

Self-hatred recalls 'my fault' as the justification for that self-blame and guilt. This occurs because 'myself' is what I know most intimately and what exists closest to me. There is abundant material to scrutinize. In essence, I make myself the scapegoat. Sometimes we blame those who are weaker than ourselves. In this case, we are making another person the left hemisphere's scapegoat. Whether we scapegoat ourselves or others, the mechanism is the same. Both are equally deplorable behaviors.

-   Many things happen 'just because' and not because of our fault.

Much of what we consider 'my fault, my mistake, my incompetence, my error' is actually not so in reality. If there is something that is actually our fault, we should neither avoid it nor turn away from it, but understand it objectively to prevent it from recurring. Surprisingly, many things 'just happen.' That is, they are 'not our fault.' We simply need to recognize and accept that 'just because' element. Without forcibly creating inaccurate reasons and justifications.

Let's consider an example. Walking down a dark path, I tripped over a stone and fell. The reason is simply that a stone happened to be there. It is not 'my fault'. Anyone passing through that dark section would inevitably trip over that stone and fall. Or perhaps I boarded a bus where someone in the back seat was coughing severely. Eventually, I caught a cold. This is not 'my fault'. It's simply because there was a person with a cold nearby. While walking through an unfamiliar village, suddenly a rabid dog leaped out from the bushes and bit my leg. In this case too, it is 'not my fault.' As it turned out, several other people walking through that village had also been bitten.

Many of our everyday or complex experiences, when examined closely, are not much different from stumbling over a rock, catching a cold, or encountering a rabid dog. We often create 'non-existent faults' and then struggle as we sink into self-blame and guilt.

If you have been suffering from and deceived by 'the left hemisphere's compulsion,' begin to recognize it and silence that meaningless chatter. Let's not torment and burden ourselves when we've done nothing wrong. This is how to exist with greater confidence and dignity.

◆ ◆ ◆

Summary

'Left hemisphere compulsion' is a psychological mechanism that frequently causes us to blame ourselves when searching for the causes of mistakes or problems. This occurs because the left hemisphere of the brain has an instinctive need to find comprehensible explanations. However, this mechanism often leads to inaccurate and unnecessary self-blame. Despite many situations simply being 'things that just happened,' we frequently look for fault within ourselves. By recognizing and stopping this habit, we can live a more confident and dignified life.

1.8 I too am an 'other' to myself who deserves fair treatment

: Most of us treat ourselves worse than we treat others

Our consciousness has the basic functions of 'objectification' and 'identification'. Objectification occurs when I become the subject of perception and regard everything outside myself as 'objects of perception.' In essence, it is the function of establishing a 'subject-object' relationship. Identification is the function of regarding an objectified entity as myself again or incorporating it into my perception of self.

In the previous text, I explained the process of self-hatred wherein one misuses this objectification function to unconsciously separate 'the capable self' and 'the incapable self' as distinct objects, and then identifies 'the capable self' as the 'real self,' thereby despising and feeling aversion toward 'the incapable self,' which is equally part of oneself. By gaining insight into this entire process, we can free ourselves from unnecessary self-hatred.

Objectification and identification themselves are not inherently negative. They are merely basic functions of consciousness that serve survival efficiency. Therefore, while we can recognize and become aware of their structure and mechanisms, we cannot eliminate them. More accurately, there is no need to eliminate them. We simply need to utilize them effectively.

Although the separation and objectification of 'my superior self' and 'my inferior self' is erroneous, it is a natural process to perceive and treat oneself as an object. All of us can 'feel ourselves'—that is, we can perceive ourselves as objects. Without requiring any special self-awareness or deliberate effort, this process is already occurring naturally in the present moment.

In our ordinary state, we fail to notice this structure. We simply think 'I am me' and consider the matter settled. But with just a bit of careful attention, we can recognize that I too am an object to myself just as others are, and that I unconsciously treat myself this way throughout daily life.

From now on, let us more clearly perceive 'the self that becomes other to me' in each moment. There's no need to forcibly experience feelings of separation or fragmentation. This isn't something that requires straining or excessive effort. It is about clearly re-perceiving a function of consciousness that until just moments ago was performed automatically and mindlessly.

The 'self' that I love, like, take pride in, hate, dislike, feel disappointed in, and regard with indifference is also an object and another entity to me. From now on, let's take good care of and treat this self fairly. After all, isn't it me, not someone else? If I treat others well, shouldn't I treat myself even better?

In reality, most of us treat 'ourselves' worse than we treat others. When something goes wrong, we are lenient with other people but uniquely harsh toward ourselves. We show ourselves no mercy whatsoever. And even when we do well, we rarely know how to praise or encourage ourselves.

Let's imagine what would happen if we treated someone else the way we treat ourselves. For even the smallest mistake, there would be endless scolding, belittlement, and attacks. Even if they excel at something, they would be extremely reluctant to acknowledge or praise it. Wouldn't such a person eventually break down? What if parents raised their child this way? It's horrifying just to imagine.

In the world, there are also many cases of the opposite. There are many people who treat others harshly while being generous only to themselves. However, this is merely how they appear when viewed from the outside. In truth, if you carefully examine the inner feelings of people who live this way, you'll discover they are never truly satisfied with themselves or at peace, lacking a healthy psychological foundation. This is because a person who is truly satisfied with themselves and values their own worth would not treat others carelessly. His apparent generosity toward himself should be viewed as a form of conscious avoidance and emotional numbness. (Their self-respect is also distorted because they have no concept of 'others'. A self that exists without acknowledging others is a pathological self.)

From now on, let us treat ourselves with the same care and love we extend to those we cherish. While we must maintain appropriate boundaries and exercise discipline where necessary, we should avoid being excessively harsh on ourselves. Don't be too harsh on yourself, don't be too rigid, and don't treat yourself with excessive objectivity. Even when offering criticism, be mindful of context, circumstances, and environment; and when praising, deliberately provide twice or three times the encouragement and support.

Not going well? It would actually be unusual if things went perfectly from the start. Since you're now doing the opposite of what you've always done, you must persevere steadily and courageously until you overcome the existing inertia and successfully change direction. Then, at a certain point when you exceed the threshold, you will naturally feel the transformation taking place.

"Yes, I made a mistake. I acknowledge that I was wrong.

But you also did your best in your own way. I recognize that clearly.

Although the outcome wasn't favorable, take responsibility for that, and independent of this setback, let's commit to excellence in our next attempt.

I believe in you.

"Wow, you're performing so admirably. This is truly characteristic of your capabilities!

This aspect of your work is exceptional by any objective standard.

I don't think I could have accomplished that much myself.

I'm truly proud of you.

Well done, once again.

Beyond these phrases, there are countless things you can say for yourself and to yourself. Keep them in mind and don't hesitate to use them generously when needed. In this one-time journey of life, should I withhold anything from myself?

Summary

We often treat ourselves more harshly than we treat others. This stems from the misuse of consciousness's 'objectification' and 'identification' functions. We perceive ourselves as objects and sometimes treat ourselves too harshly. However, we should treat ourselves fairly and kindly, as we would a cherished person. We should adopt a positive attitude toward ourselves—understanding when we make mistakes and offering more praise when we succeed.

1.9 The magical incantation: 'Nevertheless, I choose not to be consumed by it'

: The Unconscious Can Be Transformed into Consciousness

When faced with certain conditions or situations, we typically determine our emotional responses based on these circumstances. For example, we might think, 'I don't have much money, therefore I feel diminished.' Or 'I feel powerless because I lack ability' would also be appropriate. However, essentially there is no direct relationship between 'what my reality or situation is' and 'how I feel.' This is true unless one intentionally creates such a connection.

'My feelings' about 'my situation' are learned associations. This is not because one inherently should feel that way, but because one has been conditioned socially or personally 'to feel that way' through past experiences.

Is it possible to break this cycle of connection?

Of course it is. Depending on one's perspective, various approaches and methodologies are possible.

I would like to propose one such method. Find elements from your own situation or reality to complete the following phrases, then speak the completed statement as if making a declaration.

"Although I am ~, I deliberately choose not to be consumed by ~. And I freely do everything that I need to do.

You may speak this aloud or recite it in your mind. Speak repeatedly with a determined and confident mindset, in whatever manner works for you. For now, set aside concerns about whether this will actually manifest in reality. The thought 'But it's not actually true...' is merely an obstacle. Proceed as though you're already experiencing it as reality or as if you're already in that desired state. Of course, my psychological state will not transform immediately by doing this. However, the effects become increasingly evident as time passes and these affirmations are consistently practiced. Here are some examples.

Though I am short and have an unremarkable physique, I refuse to be consumed by feelings of inferiority.
And I freely do everything I need to do.

Though my knowledge may be limited, I refuse to be consumed by the psychological inhibition of feeling ignorant.
And I freely do everything I need to do.

Though I lack financial resources, I refuse to be consumed by feelings of inadequacy or poverty.
And I freely do everything I need to do.

Though I don't socialize well with others, I refuse to be consumed by feelings of alienation or loneliness.
And I freely do everything I need to do.

Although I may lack certain talents, abilities, and favorable conditions, I choose not to become consumed by self-deprecation or envy.
And I freely do everything I need to do.

Even when I truly dislike certain individuals, groups, or situations, I choose not to become consumed by feelings of anger.
And I freely do everything I need to do.

Though I clearly perceive the disorder in society, I choose not to become consumed by personal or collective feelings of defeat.

And I freely do everything I need to do.

In whatever field I engage in, even when I feel 'not there yet,' I choose not to become consumed by any sense of inadequacy, timidity, or limitation.

And I freely do everything that I need to do.

Now, let's create sentences that fit your personal situation and declare them aloud. Keep the following principle in mind.

'The unconscious can be transformed into consciousness!'

◆ ◆ ◆

Summary

Our emotional responses are primarily determined by situations, but these are merely learned associations. To break this connection, you can use the statement: 'Despite [situation], I intentionally choose not to cling to [emotional response]. And I freely do what I need to do.' By consistently repeating this declaration, we can reconstruct the connection between situations and our emotional responses. Through consistent practice, we can transform our unconscious mind.

Chapter 2: How Does Self-Hatred Transform into Aversion Toward Others?

2.1   Is That Person Really Worth Hating?

2.2   Projection is neither the 'Inner Shadow' nor malevolence

2.3   Admiration and jealousy stem from a sense of superiority

2.4   Absolving oneself by punishing others

2.5   Your projection has nothing to do with that external object

2.6   Let us transcend projection by gaining insight into the polarity of projection

2.1 Is That Person Really Worth Hating?

: Do they really deserve to receive the energy of my emotions?

Beyond self-hatred, our animosity toward others represents another significant concern in our lives. If you genuinely need to stand your ground and confront someone, if the other person needs to correct something, or if a situation requires resolution, then you should certainly take appropriate action. When legitimate intervention is required in dealing with a person or situation, you must employ all available resources. Express all thoughts, speak all necessary words, and take all required actions. However, problems arise when this approach is unwarranted. If you are harboring unnecessary hatred, different measures are required.

If you continuously harbor hatred toward someone in your daily life, and that hatred causes you emotional distress, there is something you should seriously consider for your own benefit.

Does that person truly deserve to continue receiving my hatred?

When I begin to hate someone (regardless of whether I express this hatred to them or not), from that moment onward, I feel compelled to maintain this hatred to avoid feeling wronged and to believe my actions have meaning.

In reality, hating someone is neither an act of revenge nor a method that produces the effect we desire.

To hate someone means depleting our life's energy for their sake. Hatred, too, is a form of attention. Attention requires pouring out the energy of our body and mind. When we barely have enough energy for the people and pursuits we love, why should we give our attention and life energy to those who do not deserve it?

For our own well-being, we must ask ourselves this question seriously.

Does that person truly deserve my hatred?

Do they deserve my attention?

Is it meaningful to continue giving them the energy from my life?

If they are worth it, then continue to hate them. Who would stop you, when you yourself believe they are worthy of such attention? But if it becomes clear they are not worth it, cease giving them your attention and energy. I'm simply advising you to be 'indifferent' and 'detached'. It's like throwing a bone to a dog—toss one final bit of cynicism their way and then be done with it.

Not for anyone else, but for yourself, for your own life.

No matter how much you detest excrement, you cannot simply sit there repeating, 'I hate excrement, I hate excrement!' Rather than dwelling on excrement, turn your thoughts toward flowers instead. Let us direct our attention to the truly meaningful subjects worthy of our contemplation and focus. This approach is far more beneficial.

◆ ◆ ◆

Summary

Hatred toward others is harmful to oneself. If you find yourself continuously harboring hatred for someone, you should question whether that person is truly deserving of such intense negative emotion. Hatred is an act that consumes both energy and attention. Consider whether that person is truly worth expending your life's energy on. If not, it is better to become indifferent and detached. Instead, it is more beneficial to direct your attention toward truly valuable things and people.

2.2 Projection is neither the 'Inner Shadow' nor malevolence

: Do you envy someone? You believe you are superior to that person

"Do you feel that people reject you?
In truth, it is you who does not want to engage with them.

Do you feel that someone makes you feel guilty?
In truth, it is you who does not want to accept that request.

Do you feel that everyone is watching you?
In truth, it is you who is excessively concerned with others.

Do you feel that people are trying to harm you?
In truth, it is you who harbors anger and hostility toward them.

Do you feel that you cannot do something?
In truth, you simply do not want to do it.

What is it about others that makes you despise them?
In truth, it is 'something' within yourself that you dislike.

Whom do you envy?
In truth, you actually consider yourself superior to that person.

Why do we humans so persistently view each other negatively, hate, envy, and demonize one another?

All the concepts mentioned above are related to 'projection,' one of the psychological defense mechanisms. The first part of each phrase represents a projection onto external objects, while the latter part reveals the 'Shadow' within me—the original form of that projection.

The general explanation of 'projection' is as follows: "A mechanism by which one attributes qualities inherent in oneself, yet unacceptable to consciousness, to the characteristics of other people. In essence, thinking and behaving as if one's psychological attributes exist in others rather than in oneself.

It is the process of attributing unacceptable, shocking, or discomforting thoughts, feelings, and impulses from one's inner self to others. For example, being unaware of your own anger while perceiving the other person as angry is a form of projection. Of course, the other person may genuinely be angry. Or they may not be. They might be slightly angry or significantly angry. Such judgment should be made as objectively and comprehensively as possible. However, understanding the projection phenomenon means focusing on 'the psychological structures and causes within myself' independent of external objects, while simultaneously considering all these possibilities.

The first step in resolving negative projection is addressing the 'Shadow' issue within our inner self, which constitutes the fundamental cause of projection.

Here, let us consider 'shadow-making' as 'demonization'. The reasons why the projection phenomenon manifests negatively can be analyzed as follows. First, one perceives certain aspects of one's inner self as a form of 'malevolence', and subsequently projects them onto external objects. In essence, this process involves demonizing the other person.

- Primary Illusion: Initially perceiving certain aspects of one's inner self as 'malevolence'. (This directly connects to the mechanism of self-hatred.)

● Secondary Illusion: Projecting manufactured malevolence onto external objects.

In other words, while I perceive the 'Shadow' within myself, I simultaneously fail to naturally embrace or accept it as an integral part of my being. It undeniably exists within me, yet I cannot acknowledge this reality, and consequently, I project it onto some external entity.

If this is the case, couldn't we consider two foundational approaches to ceasing this projection?

First, cease the error of perceiving the shadow aspects of your inner self as negativity or malevolence.

In essence, it is about recognizing and accepting things 'as they are.' It is merely an inherent aspect of existence and a characteristic of being. Seeing things healthily 'as they are' is itself normalization and healing.

This is also a key process in resolving the psychology of 'self-hatred,' which is our central topic. The instinctual aspects, needs, personality traits, characteristics, and desires that I possess are entirely natural for a living being. Nevertheless, due to adults' criticism and scolding during childhood, the oppression and pressure from others and society experienced while growing up, and the self-restraint mechanisms we create ourselves, we develop 'self-taboos'.

'What already exists' does not disappear even if we consider it non-existent. This is impossible from the outset. Yet we attempt this impossibility, and then we despair. This despair connects to self-hatred.

For example, the desires, anger, cravings, withdrawal, depression, and sadness we feel are not 'negative'. They are life responses and natural reactions of unity. The point is how to utilize or regulate such feelings, not to deny, suppress, or pretend they don't exist. Additionally, becoming excessively immersed in those feelings is not the answer either. Such absorption produces no positive effects and instead creates only adverse consequences. Both reactions ultimately result in projecting unresolved internal issues onto external objects.

Second, it is recognizing when we are projecting onto others or external circumstances.

It is about gaining the insight that the Shadow or malevolence within me is not inherently evil, and that the negativity and malevolence I perceive in others is also not 'their true nature or state.' Therefore, the first step is to stop projecting negativity onto others that does not actually exist within them. Of course, there may be cases where the other person does indeed possess negative qualities. Even in such cases, it is important not to perceive or attribute negativity that exceeds the person's actual negative qualities.

For example, if a person's negativity is measured on a scale where 100 represents the maximum intensity, the current state of the other person might objectively be around 30. However, we must cease perceiving it as 70-80, which happens when 'the projection of my inner self and demonization of the other person' distorts our perception. Due to these exaggerated assessments, our emotions and reactions inevitably intensify. Even situations we could normally handle appropriately may trigger disproportionate responses or significant conflicts. Ultimately, both ourselves and others suffer from these unnecessary conflicts.

While it is important to stop the second illusion, for a fundamental solution, one must first clearly gain insight into, recognize, and notice the first illusion of 'the malevolence in my inner self.' If you cannot healthily accept yourself, you cannot fully accept the external world either. This is because internally and externally are not completely separate as we think they are in essence.

The key is to recognize that it was not 'negative' in the first place. In other words, the various emotions, feelings, thoughts, and reactions within me exist naturally for valid reasons; they are not things that should be eliminated or denied. Desires, needs, fears, anger, anxiety... all of these are merely labels that we humans have attached, having nothing to do with the original emotions and feelings themselves. The various needs, desires, and emotions I feel are simply natural 'responses and cries of life.' The fact that it exists and that we feel it is not problematic whatsoever. Rather, the essence lies in how we respond to and process these feelings. This isn't suggesting that you should act on all your feelings and desires unconditionally, but rather that you should find and implement the most wise solution.

If we prematurely determine that these feelings 'should not be felt, should not be contemplated, should not exist,' then all subsequent processes and interventions will inevitably be misaligned.

When the issue of 'the Shadow within me' is resolved, the projection problem is almost solved. This is because they are phenomena connected by cause and effect. If I properly embrace, accept, acknowledge, and process my inner feelings, desires, emotions, and thoughts, I no longer have anything to project onto external objects and others. Or even if projections continue to occur externally as before, they no longer hold significant importance. When we become unconcerned with the projection process itself, the presence or absence of projections ceases to be problematic.

To resolve projection, it is better to first address the issues of 'myself' and 'my inner self' rather than focusing on external objects and others. This means resolving 'my inner shadow' issues. The goal isn't to eliminate or fix the shadow, but to recognize that the shadow is not truly a shadow at all. So it begins with warmly and generously accepting and embracing myself. This allows us to finally transcend the aspects we've misinterpreted as shadow. When we embrace it, we can transcend it. These are two aspects of the same phenomenon.

This process is not an easy one. We carry habits that have accumulated over decades. These manifest as mental, conscious, and behavioral patterns. Since this work involves recognizing, halting, and transforming these patterns, it will require both time and dedicated effort. However, this doesn't mean it's impossible or unattainable. The very act of 'beginning' is already a form of 'completion,' provided you continue without stopping midway. The destination is absolutely certain.

◆ ◆ ◆

Summary

Projection is a psychological defense mechanism in which we attribute our unacceptable characteristics to others. This includes the process of demonizing one's inner 'Shadow' and projecting it outward. To resolve this, one must first accept their Shadow aspects as they are, without viewing them negatively. Second, one must recognize and cease projections onto others. When inner issues are resolved, projection problems naturally dissipate as well. This process requires time and effort, but with consistent practice, it can certainly be achieved.

2.3 Admiration and jealousy stem from a sense of superiority

: Superiority and inferiority complexes arise simultaneously

Throughout life, everyone experiences envy or jealousy toward others. This isn't limited to immature children. Regardless of age, this psychological response is unavoidable even for those who have established themselves as authorities in their field. Though people may pretend otherwise externally, when someone of similar or superior ability receives more attention or achieves greater success, everyone experiences feelings of envy and jealousy.

There are times when envy and jealousy can have positive effects. In many cases, 'jealousy becomes my strength,' motivating us to work harder or exert greater effort. But ultimately, these emotions ruin our mood and drain our energy. This occurs because envy and jealousy are fundamentally negative psychological states.

Do you wish to stop experiencing envy and jealousy? However, these feelings don't simply cease merely because we will them to. If you sincerely wish to liberate yourself from envy and jealousy, you must employ appropriate psychological methods.

There is something we need to understand first.

The fact that the original emotion behind admiration and jealousy is actually a superiority complex.

In projection theory, the shadow (the original archetypal emotion) of admiration and jealousy is viewed as a 'superiority complex'. This might sound strange at first hearing. When we admire or feel jealous of someone, it typically occurs when we feel that we are lacking or insufficient in some way, which seems to be related to an inferiority complex. But a superiority complex? How can that be?

We feel envy and jealousy when we are dissatisfied with

ourselves or our circumstances and conditions. In essence, we fail to view ourselves as adequate. Alternatively, it may stem from desire. It arises from our longing to possess what others have.

Both 'feelings of inadequacy' and 'desire' are consequences, not causes. Therefore, addressing feelings of inadequacy or relinquishing desire will not necessarily stop or eliminate envy and jealousy. This is precisely why most efforts to eliminate envy ultimately fail. It is because we attempt to change the result rather than addressing the underlying cause. The true causes of emotions or expressions that are projected outward remain hidden like 'shadows.' In reality, they aren't even hidden—we simply fail to notice them.

When we remain unaware of our original emotions and their causes, we continue to project irrelevant content externally. Why? Simply because we 'do not know.' It is similar to when children throw tantrums and their crying does not stop because we fail to notice their real needs and instead offer them something irrelevant. 'Envy and jealousy' projected toward external objects are, in a sense, instances of throwing tantrums at ourselves. In such moments, one fails to recognize their authentic emotions, desires, or intentions, and instead continues to express something entirely unrelated.

From this point forward, we will work on recognizing the fundamental emotions underlying envy and jealousy. This is the process of self-acknowledgment. The more accurately you recognize it, the more projection is destined to gradually disappear—like a child who becomes quiet with satisfaction after throwing a tantrum. Though not an easy process, it is achievable.

- Superiority complex and inferiority complex occur simultaneously

Let us quietly examine our minds. When we envy someone who possesses something desirable or finds themselves in a favorable situation, our typical response is, 'Ah, I want to have that too,' or 'I wish I could be like that.'

This is not our true mind. It's '(not you but) I am the one who could have it, who deserves to have it.' In short, it becomes 'I am the one who is truly superior.'

If I consider myself deeply inadequate, insufficient, and undeserving, I wouldn't even contemplate wanting to possess it or aspire to become that way. Isn't there a case where something seems like an 'insurmountable wall'—a barrier impossible to cross—so you don't even feel envy or jealousy? You don't even dare to attempt it from the outset.

Jealousy is an emotion that arises when there's a high possibility that I could possess something or when the gap between having and not having is not too large, while envy might be seen as occurring when that possibility seems more distant. Though individual differences exist, this generally holds true. Jealousy emerges when our internal superiority complex is stronger, while envy manifests when it is weaker.

From now on, let's become self-aware whenever we experience envy, covetousness, or jealousy. 'Ah, I am experiencing a superiority complex right now.' I'm thinking, 'I deserve that state, that person, that gift, that championship—not them.' This is never an inferiority complex or mere desire. It's a superiority complex. Let's not forget this.

You might find yourself thinking: 'Isn't a superiority complex fundamentally beneficial for me? Why should this be problematic?'

There is a reason for this concern. It's because superiority and inferiority complexes invariably occur as a pair.

And it's not limited to just superiority and inferiority complexes.

All emotions or concepts that we possess occur in pairs. Just as a magnet simultaneously has N-S poles, and electricity simultaneously has negative and positive poles. A superiority complex cannot exist separately from an inferiority complex.

In other words, the 'superiority-inferiority complex' pair does not consist of separately existing entities, but rather represents 'two polarities existing as one body'. In fact, they are a single unity. They appear as a pair and disappear as a pair. Usually, we tend to focus on and feel only one of the two, mistakenly believing that the counterpart does not exist. However, inferiority and superiority are shadow concepts of each other. When one manifests, the other merely becomes a hidden shadow, yet both continue to operate equally.

If superiority complex and inferiority complex appear simultaneously as a pair, there must be a 'something' that could be considered their core entity or body—a body with two faces. We must see this clearly to properly address our problems. What constitutes this body?

The true essence of the 'superiority-inferiority complex' pair is the pervasive mindset of comparison and discrimination. In other words, superiority and inferiority emerge from our tendency to compare and discriminate. Without comparison and discrimination, neither superiority nor inferiority can exist. Therefore, when experiencing envy and jealousy, one should recognize the underlying feelings of superiority and inferiority, understanding that these arise from one's own mind of comparison and discrimination.

Aren't comparison and discrimination natural? Is there anyone among humans who doesn't compare? Don't we need to make comparisons to understand differences?

That's correct. However, there's just one thing we need to properly understand. The 'comparison and discrimination' that generate feelings of superiority and inferiority are not part of our original nature. In their purest form, they are merely 'dispassionate measurements.' In other words, it's the act of neutrally assessing which thing is longer or shorter, heavier or lighter, brighter or darker, more suitable or unsuitable, and so forth. Such measurements are certainly necessary, and the more accurate they are, the better. The ability to measure is precisely what humans excel at compared to other animals.

The problem is that we repeatedly contaminate objective measurements with subjective comparisons and discrimination. We unnecessarily add 'like/dislike' judgments and overlay reactions of 'superior/inferior'. When this intensifies, it extends into 'obsession/aversion'. Of course, attaching 'like/dislike' emotions to measurement results is not something to be criticized. Rather, it is a natural response. We make our choices based on these responses. Even an amoeba, a single-celled organism, retreats and navigates around obstacles while crawling along the ground, and moves toward and attaches itself to beneficial things.

The problem arises when we apply the 'like/dislike' dichotomy in situations where such judgments are unnecessary. Or when we remain trapped in 'like/dislike' evaluations even in circumstances where we should transcend these judgments or need not be bound by them.

For instance, someone else is dating a desirable partner whom I might envy. To label something as 'good' implies that an evaluation has already taken place. For instance, the abundance or scarcity of wealth, or the handsomeness or unattractiveness of one's face. It simply ends there. It means having a bit more money or having a more harmonious facial appearance. The other person has found such a partner.

So what? Does that determine me and my life? Clearly not. That is merely 'their business.' Unless I make it my business, it has nothing to do with me. Using their affairs to determine my value and the worth of my life brings no benefit whatsoever. Why must we transform that simple 'measurement' into 'comparison', connecting it to superiority and inferiority, ultimately creating envy and jealousy? There is absolutely no reason to do so.

Most people don't stop at dry measurement but develop sticky feelings of comparison and discrimination that adhere to their perceptions. This becomes the foundation from which the positive and negative poles of superiority and inferiority emerge. The superiority complex I feel hides in the Shadow. 'I should be enjoying that.' Unconsciously, one conceals the feeling that 'I should be the one to possess this.' Ultimately, the remaining envy and jealousy are projected onto others, causing one to repeatedly experience negative emotions and energy depletion. This occurs because projection is essentially a 'fabricated, inauthentic emotion.'

Had we journeyed this far together, resolution would likely have occurred naturally. If you wish to continue experiencing and utilizing envy and jealousy, you are certainly free to do so. But what can one do about the mental strain and psychological energy that is depleted because of this? Therefore, if you wish to cease the projections that cause you distress and drain your mental energy, try the following approach.

From now on, when feelings of envy and jealousy arise, immediately recognize them as projections of your internal superiority complex. Projection is an inauthentic emotion. In reality, I am not genuinely experiencing envy and jealousy. Instead, let us become aware of and acknowledge the underlying emotion—the superiority complex itself.

Furthermore, let us understand that this superiority complex represents one pole in the unnecessary spectrum of 'comparison and discrimination'. Finally, let us recognize that comparison and discrimination are not inherent qualities but contaminations of objective measurement. In its pure form, it is simply measurement. There is nothing wrong or problematic about measurement itself. We can utilize it effectively when necessary.

When we intentionally recognize that the true nature of 'the comparing and discriminating mind' is actually 'the mind of objective measurement and discernment,' and refrain from adding unnecessary emotional elements, feelings of superiority and inferiority toward others cease to arise. Long things are simply long and short things are short; neither is superior nor inferior to the other. And even if these feelings arise, let us no longer be concerned with them. This is because they hold little significance except when necessary. Even if feelings of superiority complex and inferiority complex continue to emerge for some time, let us utilize them only as needed and disregard them otherwise.

To summarize once more: even if these feelings arise, there is no need to eliminate, deny, or attempt to stop them—simply recognize their true nature as thoughts of 'superiority-inferiority.' Recognizing that the foundation is a mindset of 'sticky comparison and discrimination'. And seeing 'comparison and discrimination' for what they truly are: 'objective measurement and discernment.' Thus becoming unbothered by their presence. Thus allowing them to gradually fade away on their own. This is the path forward.

I won't claim this process is easy. However, it is a method that works when applied consistently. It is a definitive method to free oneself from envy and jealousy, to transcend comparisons of superiority and inferiority. Therefore, let us work on this together until we succeed. Even with obstacles along the way, if you neither give up nor stop, you will eventually reach your destination. That is the power of our mind. If you consistently maintain your determination, it need not be so difficult after all.

◆ ◆ ◆

Summary

The true root of jealousy and envy is, paradoxically, a superiority complex. This originates from the 'viscous' mindset of comparison and discrimination. Superiority complex and inferiority complex always manifest together, both arising from unnecessary 'comparison and discrimination.' To resolve this issue, one must recognize that feelings of jealousy or envy are projections of one's superiority complex. Furthermore, one must understand that these emotions stem from mere 'dry measurement and judgment' of others. By understanding the true nature of these emotions, one can avoid unnecessary comparisons and discrimination, ultimately freeing oneself from jealousy and envy.

2.4 Absolving oneself by punishing others
: Mirror of the Shadow - Understanding Negative Projection

Earlier, I mentioned that projection toward the outside (especially negative projection) occurs due to misunderstanding of the shadow elements within myself. This time, we will identify the mechanism of 'negative projection' that captures us and examine how we can transition to 'healthy projection'.

Let's consider an example. Someone appears extremely cowardly, and I dislike both the cowardice and that cowardly person. However, (regardless of whether that person is actually cowardly or not) such 'element of cowardice' exists within me, and I am suppressing or avoiding it because I cannot acknowledge or accept that element. That element clearly exists as a normal part of myself or of human nature, yet I am repressing it as a 'Shadow' because I cannot accept its presence.

More importantly, labeling it as 'cowardice' is a misunderstanding. In reality, it might not be cowardice but simply 'caution'. Or perhaps it is a form of 'rational response' in its own right. Nevertheless, because I cannot acknowledge or permit its existence, I view it as a shadow and consequently repress, avoid, or ignore it. If I could simply accept it with equanimity, it would cease to be problematic.

In such a state, if one perceives these elements in another person, regardless of what that person is actually like, one immediately concludes, 'That person is cowardly. I dislike that.' Of course, that person may or may not actually be cowardly. What is important here is not that person but myself and my inner self.

The same mechanism operates when a sexually conservative person feels rejection or aversion toward a sexually liberated person. Unable to acknowledge 'the pursuit or desire for sexual freedom' within their inner self, one lives experiencing such internal tension both consciously and unconsciously, ultimately projecting it externally. It is the act of self-absolution through 'punishing' the target with hatred, anger, or aversion. Of course, this is merely a temporary solution with nothing actually resolved, and the pattern continues to repeat itself in the future.

Projection can be divided into 'negative projection' and 'healthy projection'. The classification system that divides projection into negative projection and healthy projection already exists in established literature, and should be understood as a useful methodology rather than something absolute or unique. Even this distinction alone can provide considerable help in resolving the problem of negative projection that complicates our daily lives. Of course, ultimately, the goal should be to recognize the true nature of any projection and fundamentally liberate ourselves from projection altogether.

'Negative projection' occurs when we place all causes and elements 'outside' ourselves without recognizing that we are projecting. This leads to becoming immersed in projection and blaming others. Furthermore, negative projection is primarily accompanied by 'emotional reactions'. Of course, not all emotional reactions constitute negative projections. There are many healthy and normal emotional responses. Those are simply projections. In contrast, negative projection occurs when one fails to properly perceive and understand the true state, appearance, or intentions of others or external circumstances, instead experiencing them as 'distorted states, appearances, and intentions' due to one's internal elements. One fails to accurately perceive the other person and the situation, resulting in unnecessary and inefficient emotional, cognitive, and behavioral responses.

'Healthy projection' is recognizing the possibility of projection while we perceive and understand external objects and others. That is, while seeing and feeling the same things in external objects, one becomes fully self-aware that there are elements being projected from within oneself. Therefore, regarding the emotions, behaviors, intentions, and thoughts of the object that one perceives or interprets, one initially interprets according to their projection, while simultaneously maintaining awareness that 'other possibilities' always exist. That is, actively considering that what I am feeling right now may not be exactly as it appears. Therefore, positive projection does not become immersed in the projection itself and produces fewer negative emotional reactions. Of course, even healthy projection does not mean that emotional reactions should be completely absent. Emotional reactions are natural in any form of projection. Healthy projection differs in that I do not become excessively immersed or swept away by it, and it does not unnecessarily influence my judgment.

From one perspective, projection appears to be connected to the functioning of 'mirror neurons,' which enable us to directly experience or mimic the emotions and actions of others. In other words, projection is linked to our capacity for external learning and empathy. Furthermore, it may represent a fundamental perceptual function of the brain, which will be elaborated upon in the following section. Therefore, the projection phenomenon in its broader sense should be understood as a neutral and valuable 'tool,' rather than as a pathological condition. Our responsibility, then, is to comprehend its function and structure as thoroughly as possible and to utilize it effectively.

Summary

This text explains the concepts of negative projection and healthy projection. Negative projection occurs when we project our unrecognized shadow elements onto others, while healthy projection involves understanding the external world while remaining conscious of our tendency to project. Projection may be related to mirror neurons and can be viewed as a fundamental cognitive function underlying our capacity for learning and empathy. The goal is to understand projection and utilize it effectively.

2.5 Your projection has nothing to do with that external object

: Beyond the Shadow - Expanding Our Understanding of Projection

There is a common point of confusion when people first encounter projection theory. When there is someone I dislike, hate, or feel aversion toward, projection theory promptly asserts that the characteristics I attribute to that person actually exist within myself. To this, we often respond, 'That's not true. It seems forced' or perhaps 'Yes, that could be possible,' though the former response is more common. Even those who partially accept it might think, 'There might be some truth to that. But is it really that straightforward?' Yet it fails to erase the lingering question: 'Is that all there is to it?'

There is a valid reason for this doubt. This is because that may not be the entirety of the projection phenomenon. In other words, it represents only a partial explanation. Of course, in general projection, especially negative projection, the mechanism of denying one's shadow—the negative aspects within oneself—and overlaying it onto external objects is substantially accurate. By raising this process to consciousness, one can avoid experiencing unnecessary projections and emotional difficulties.

Beyond this, we now need to examine the human projection mechanism from a broader perspective. That is, we must understand not just negative projection but the projection phenomenon in its entirety. This means comprehending projection not only as a processing mechanism for the 'Inner shadow' but as our fundamental mechanism of perception through which we understand the world.

Attempting to 'unconditionally' stop or eliminate negative projection can inadvertently lead to avoidance, suppression, or repression, and does not constitute a fundamental solution. Certainly, for the quality of our lives and relationships, we need to free ourselves from negative projection. However, it is preferable to achieve this through deep understanding and insight about projection rather than unconditional avoidance. The more clearly and deeply we understand the projection phenomenon, the better we will be able to utilize it. This is because understanding promotes effective application.

In this article and the next, I will attempt to complement and expand upon the existing limited interpretations of the projection phenomenon using two perspectives. This is not a matter of right versus wrong. This is because when a phenomenon occurs, there can be various interpretations of it. The key factors are accuracy, precision, and utility.

In this article, I will reinterpret the projection phenomenon using findings from neuroscience research. The core perspective is that in human perception, 'information that enters from the outside and is perceived' and 'information that is projected from the inside to the outside' are essentially unrelated.

- A Neuroscientific Understanding of the Projection Phenomenon

The fourth episode of the BBC2 six-part documentary 'Brain Story' titled "First among Equals," which was also broadcast in Korea, features a case study of a man named 'Kevin'. This case study demonstrates that 'what we observe externally' and 'what we perceive in the mind (brain)' can be completely separate processes.

Kevin suffers from object recognition disorder resulting from an accident. In the documentary, scientists ask Kevin to draw a bicycle. Inside Kevin's brain, the image of a bicycle remains, so he draws a picture of a bicycle. Nevertheless, when asked what he just drew, he answers, 'I don't know.'

Even though the object before him is the bicycle he just visualized in his mind and even drew, he claims not to recognize it because he has a perception disorder that prevents him from processing external information. Even so, this remains logically difficult to comprehend. Even if one develops a perception disorder regarding external objects, how could they fail to recognize a picture they themselves just drew? It's not even complex. Yet such a connection simply does not occur!

The researcher's interpretation is as follows. The two perception processes—from external to internal and from internal to external—are completely separate entities with no direct correlation between them. Under normal circumstances, we connect these two processes to complete our perception, but this is explained as a kind of 'temporary connection' or 'random association,' not because the two processes are actually related to each other. It seems there is no logical explanation for the 'perception of the world' that we hold.

This is a reasonable and valid inference based on observed phenomena rather than an established principle. However, even beyond Kevin's case, careful observation of our daily lives reveals inconsistencies or disconnections between 'external objects' and 'internal perception.' While we often dismiss these as exceptional phenomena, from a neuroscience perspective, such inconsistencies might actually represent our natural state.

For example, there are instances when we make errors in judgment about people or situations we encounter. Sometimes we err due to carelessness, and even when we observe something with reasonable accuracy, misunderstandings or misinterpretations can still occur. In either case, a discrepancy arises between the 'external object' and our 'internal perception'. In some instances, despite believing we have grasped something with complete accuracy, discrepancies or irrelevancies may still exist. These discrepancies between external reality and internal perception are phenomena we frequently experience in our daily lives.

There could be objections to this perspective. One might argue that such cases are not 'essential discrepancies' as described in the above experiment, but rather 'situational discrepancies' that occur due to inaccurate understanding. That's correct. They are clearly different types. However, there may be some connection between them. Perhaps the situational discrepancy between 'external objects' and 'internal perception' that we experience might be a partial manifestation of the original essential discrepancy. While this is also merely a conjecture, being mindful that we can commit 'discrepancy errors' at any time proves useful in numerous aspects of self-understanding. This is because it has the effect of preventing us from blindly following misconceptions or misunderstandings.

When our impressions and evaluations about a certain object or situation are judged to be incorrect, we typically assume that 'we made a wrong judgment' and consider the problem resolved by correcting our perception of that external object. However, sometimes even that corrected perception can be another misconception or misunderstanding. In other words, the discrepancy occurs again. Usually, through several rounds of correction, we gradually narrow down the errors and eventually arrive at an almost accurate perception. Strictly speaking, one could argue that this process has no definitive end. In other words, the perceptions we organize represent merely a 'relative alignment,' not an 'absolute correlation.'

This text is not asserting that the fundamental discrepancy between 'information entering from outside' and 'information emanating from within' is absolute. Rather, it presents one possibility grounded in neuroscientific discoveries. Furthermore, this does not suggest that all our 'perceptions' are entirely erroneous or should be dismissed. Such an extreme position is unnecessary. Even if there is no direct correlation in essence, the 'utility' of perception created by connecting these two pieces of information nonetheless exists. Thanks to this utility, human civilization has been created and maintained, and individuals can navigate their existence day by day, moment by moment.

It can be profoundly useful to recognize that our perception process, which seemingly naturally connects external and internal information, is not as absolute as we might assume.

Above all, acknowledging that certain perceptions may not be absolute allows 'errors that occur from treating incorrect perceptions as absolute truths' to be more easily identified and corrected. It is not an exaggeration to say that the suffering and distress experienced by both individuals and groups largely stem from an inability to acknowledge or accept the 'possibility that their perceptions might be incorrect.' While it is our perception that is flawed, not our essential self, we fall into error by identifying ourselves with our perceptions and treating the results of these perceptions as absolute truth.

From this understanding, we can develop a new interpretation of the projection phenomenon that we originally intended to discuss. The projection discussed here refers to projection in a considerably expanded sense—encompassing not only negative projection that is externalized to deny the shadow aspects of one's inner self, but literally 'all perception' that humans superimpose from their internal world onto external reality. And as we examined earlier, the projections we overlay onto external objects may, in fact, have no direct connection with those external objects. We simply perceive them as connected in that way.

When we free ourselves from the absolute connection between external objects and internal perception, we no longer need to unconditionally depend on our projections onto external objects. When the usefulness is high, we can connect and utilize them; when the usefulness is low, we can separate them. In conclusion, we can liberate ourselves from both our own projections and those of others to that extent.

◆ ◆ ◆

Summary

This text expands our understanding of psychological projection. Based on neuroscience research, it suggests that there may be no inherent connection between external information and our internal projections. Recognizing that our cognitive processes are not absolute helps us identify and correct errors in our thinking. This enables a broader interpretation of projection, allowing us to work with projections more freely by releasing ourselves from the presumed absolute connection between external objects and internal perception.

2.6 Let us transcend projection by gaining insight into the polarity of projection

: Dissolving 'Black and White' Distinctions in Our Perception

In a sense, existing projection theories have all addressed only the resulting phenomena. This is not to say they are incorrect or insufficient, but rather that their observational perspective was limited in this way. A certain conscious phenomenon occurs, but this has been overlooked in favor of focusing on the subsequent phenomenon or result. This implies that there exists a conscious phenomenon that precedes and forms the foundation for the resultant projection phenomenon.

The existing projection theory is valid to a certain extent, yet somewhat problematic in other respects. For instance, let us suppose that I currently despise someone's behavior. As we examined earlier, two stages of conscious phenomena occur in this situation. The first is feeling or perceiving some aspect within myself that I dislike, and the second is projecting this onto an external object.

Now, there exists a 'background consciousness phenomenon' that facilitates the occurrence of these two phenomena.

It is precisely 'perception that occurs in pairs.' For convenience, we could simply express this as 'black-and-white thinking.'

For instance, let's say we are observing the color 'black' in our external environment. In order to perceive it as black, we must have the perception of its opposite, 'white,' within our cognitive framework. The perception of these two colors is, naturally, already constructed from past experiences. If we observe the black outside without having an internal perception of white, we might sense it on a feeling level, but we would not cognitively recognize it as 'black.' Perhaps when we first saw the color white as children, we did not perceive it as 'white' but rather as some kind of 'raw sensation.' This would have been true not only for colors but for all physical sensations of objects. Just feeling 'Ah, something exists' without the concept of 'that is something.'

After becoming familiar with both 'white' and 'black,' and learning that they are respectively 'something with a feeling opposite to the dark color' and 'something with a feeling opposite to the white color,' we finally acquire a complete sensory and conceptual contrast between black and white.

When the perception of the 'black-white' distinction emerges and concepts are attached to it, we subsequently begin to regard black as inherently 'black' and white as inherently 'white'. We feel and believe that this distinction is factual and absolute.

Strictly speaking, this is merely a form of 'post-interpretation'. This is because there was a moment when we first encountered 'black' and 'white' when we neither felt nor perceived them as we do now. What we feel afterward is not black or white itself, but merely the constructs and labels we have imposed upon them.

Whether we perceive it as black or not, 'that object' existed as it was and continues to exist independently of our perception. Even now as you read this text, if you look at something black before you as you did in the first moment—that is, if you do not view it as black in contrast to the feeling of 'white'—it is no longer perceived as the black we know. This applies even to the feeling itself.

(Feelings do not change immediately. This is because existing feelings in the brain and consciousness change through repetition and training. However, 'perception' can change instantly regardless of feelings. For example, it is like when you wake up from a nap at home during a holiday afternoon, see the dimly lit surroundings and think it is the next morning, until a family member informs you that you have merely awakened from a nap. The 'perception' that it was 'the next morning' shifts to 'the same day evening' in a very brief moment. Similarly, as a kind of thought experiment, you can attempt to directly observe something black or another color before you without the perception that 'it is black.' If you experience even a slightly unfamiliar sensation, you have succeeded. This resembles the moment when we temporarily blank out because we suddenly cannot recall the name of something we ordinarily know well.)

In the world, there exist countless such 'perceptions of objects'. Of course, many qualities don't necessarily contrast as starkly as 'black and white'. However, in any case, when we examine the details, we can observe that perception is constructed through similar structures. We distinguish various colors because when we see one color, we simultaneously maintain an intuitive awareness of other colors. This principle applies to all physical sensations of objects, including texture.

Perception of more abstract objects also develops and occurs through the same expansive process. Perceptual distinctions become increasingly complex not only through structures where two polarities contrast, but as already established paired concepts intertwine with one another. This resembles how in Eastern philosophy, the primordial Taiji divides into Yin and Yang, which then continue to branch into the Four Symbols, Eight Trigrams, and 16 Hexagrams.

Among these concepts, the element essential for understanding projection is precisely the initial formation of 'contrasting perception'—what we call 'Black-and-white thinking.' If I project 'cowardice' onto some external object, a sense of 'righteousness' simultaneously arises within me. In this instance, these two elements exist to support each other. 'Cowardice' is the perception of 'cowardice' that arises within me, independent of any external object. And when it occurs, just as a sense of blackness is supported by a sense of whiteness, a perception of 'righteousness' exists simultaneously within me.

Within the dual concept or dual recognition of the 'cowardice-righteousness spectrum,' I only accept righteousness while being unable to accept cowardice. These two are like the poles of a magnet that cannot be separated—'a unity with two polarities' that emerges, moves, and disappears as one—yet we attempt to acknowledge only one polarity as if such separation were possible. The two are essentially no different, but we artificially designate one as good and one as bad, then reject one while embracing the other.

I attempt to retain 'righteousness,' which I consider good, while discarding 'cowardice.' The rejected negative polarity remains dormant until a plausible external target appears, at which point it becomes projected onto that target. Thus, he becomes 'the coward' while I become 'the righteous one,' allowing me to comfortably despise and dislike his cowardice. I now perceive myself as safe.

This entire process is, strictly speaking, an 'illusion' and 'imagination' of our consciousness. The 'cowardice-righteousness spectrum' does not consist of separate entities but rather a pair that emerges simultaneously—like conjoined twin brothers. Though their polarities clearly differ, they cannot be divided. They arise together and fade together. This distinction must be clearly understood. We must recognize that this is not merely theoretical but reflects our actual perceptual processes.

Once we become aware of this, several 'subsequent processes' will naturally unfold. This insight can serve as the most fundamental method for resolving negative projections onto others and the external world. It involves gaining insight into both polarities of projection and ultimately transcending projection altogether.

I am by no means suggesting that this model is absolute. This is because articulating human consciousness and the processes or structures of perception with the clarity of mathematics or physics remains somewhat elusive. Fortunately, as recent neuroscience research has advanced remarkably, various aspects of cognitive science are gradually being revealed in greater detail, allowing us to explain the structure, identity, and essence of human consciousness and perception through neurophysiological mechanisms. We too must utilize these research findings and discoveries.

Even if certain aspects have not yet been discovered or explained by neuroscience, psychology, or philosophy, we cannot claim to be completely ignorant of our own consciousness and perceptual phenomena. Consciousness or perception phenomena are not separate from us; rather, we are both the owners of these phenomena and their products. We are precisely that itself.

In this respect, 'experiential observation and insight' prove most valuable. As the subjects of consciousness and perception phenomena, we must carefully observe and gain insight into what we are experiencing. Of course, the process, content, and conclusions may differ from person to person, but we can extract common elements by engaging in dialogue with one another. Why? This is because conscious phenomena and perceptions are common experiences shared by all of us.

Now, we come to the final section.

How are 'black-and-white thinking' or the 'cowardice-righteousness spectrum distinction' and their dual formations, dual concepts, and dual recognitions useful in resolving negative projections toward others? When negative projections toward someone cause suffering for ourselves, distress for others, and create relationship problems, what can we do to prevent these issues from escalating further?

It is about clearly perceiving 'the polarity of projection.' Additionally, recognizing that it is ultimately a single construct.

For example, when we perceive cowardice in another person, we are actually sensing the cowardice within ourselves, which coexists with our own sense of righteousness. By recognizing this dynamic and determining that external projection is unnecessary, we can release both the righteousness and cowardice within ourselves when observing others. The goal is not to stop feeling these emotions, but rather to feel them while maintaining a mindful detachment. It involves carefully observing what feelings arise within me as I look at the other person. In essence, it means 'observing and experiencing the other person while setting aside my internal sense of justice and perceptions of cowardice.'

If this effort succeeds, you will no longer perceive the other person as cowardly. Or even if you do, that perception will gradually fade. This is not about forcing yourself to feel or think that 'the other person is not cowardly.' Such forced perception will fail. Why? Just as when told 'Don't think of a banana,' one inevitably thinks of a banana, no matter how much one tries to believe 'he is not a coward,' the distinction of 'cowardice' still exists, and the underlying feeling of the 'cowardice-righteousness spectrum' within oneself remains unchanged. This represents the area where people most frequently err in emotional processing, emotional regulation, and addressing emotional issues. Therefore, whether addressing problems of projection or emotion, the genuine solution lies in resolving this fundamental issue of the 'cowardice-righteousness spectrum'. It is about identifying and resolving the issues of bipolarity, dual formation, and dual recognition.

There is another point that requires caution. It is not about completely erasing or eliminating this 'cowardice-righteousness spectrum'. This is not only impossible from the outset, but forcing such an attempt would merely result in mechanisms of 'repression, suppression, avoidance, and denial'. One might believe their negative projections have disappeared, but these projections remain embedded in the substratum of consciousness, continuing to exert their influence. Rather, one only becomes more distressed thinking, 'I eliminated it, so why does it continue to cause problems?' or 'Why won't it disappear?'

It is not about erasing, eliminating, or pretending it doesn't exist, but about recognizing this fundamental structure and process. It's about becoming aware of it. Properly. The more clearly you become aware of it, the more the influence of projection diminishes. You gradually become liberated from its effects. You're not free because it has disappeared, but because its presence no longer affects you. Why? Because I understand what this phenomenon is and its true nature.

To emphasize once more, one perceives and distinguishes both 'black-white' and 'cowardice-righteousness,' but simply utilizes them according to necessity. There is no need to do anything about blackness or cowardice. And even when it is unnecessary, useless, or causes pain, the distinction remains clear, but one becomes less rigidly attached to it. This is also the principle behind the common saying, 'It's okay to be okay, and it's okay to not be okay.' There is a profound difference between acting with knowledge of this principle versus acting without it.

◆ ◆ ◆

Summary

This text explains how to transcend projection through insights into the polarity of projection. Our perception is composed of pairs of contrasting concepts, which is explained as 'black-and-white distinction perception.' To resolve negative projection, one must recognize this bipolarity and realize that it is merely a construct. The goal is not to completely eliminate these pairs, but to clearly recognize their structure and process, and utilize them effectively as needed.

Chapter 3: 'I' Am Not a Being Determined by Content

3.1   Identity is a feeling, not content

3.2   Will you become an existence living according to the scenario, or will you become the subject who creates the scenario?

3.3   Why do we need recognition from others and the world?

3.4   What we truly fear is not 'decision' but 'experience'

3.5   We need not rush to be 'ultimately right'

3.6   There are no bad personalities, only unskilled masters

3.7   The essence of life lies not in its content but in its utilization

3.8   The story of The Girl who suddenly discovered 'herself' one day

3.1 Identity is a feeling, not content

: The Essence of Ego Identity

When looking at a person, we usually see their 'content.' Who they are, what they do, what past they have, what achievements they've attained—if they're a student, which school they attend and whether they excel academically; if they're an employee, which company they work for and their annual salary; if they're an artist, what works they've created and awards they've received; if they're a scholar, what theories they've developed and what research they've successfully completed, and so on.

All attempts to define someone's identity through content inevitably fail.

Why is that? Because a person's true identity has no relation to such content. What one has done and who one is now are merely secondary considerations. Numerous issues related to self-identity, self-efficacy, self-confidence, and self-esteem originate from this fundamental misunderstanding. It stems from attempting to define a person's identity through content when identity cannot be determined by content. The two representative 'contents' that we commonly mistake for identity are 'who am I' and 'what am I doing'. The 'comparison' that troubles us also stems from these two factors. If identity were determined by the content of one's life, it would be like an actor trying to define their existential purpose off-stage through the role they perform. Whether you consider yourself inadequate or excellent, the outcome remains the same. I am not an existence defined by 'who I am' or 'what I am doing'. While I use and utilize these aspects, I exist wholly and completely independent of them.

Identity is more a 'feeling' than content. What kind of feeling are we referring to? It is the unwavering 'sense of solidity, confidence, and dignity' that one naturally develops about oneself. Being confident and dignified just as you are now, even with nothing, even doing nothing! And remarkably, it doesn't matter even if you aren't confident and dignified. While aspects of identity may be filled or expressed through one's attributes, its essence lies in this 'feeling, this lived experience'.

What should be emphasized most to kindergarten and elementary school children is none other than 'unconditional self-esteem'. Not the belief that 'I am a worthy individual' only if I excel at something, possess more things, or triumph in competition, but rather the inherent feeling that 'I am a worthy individual' regardless of these external factors. This requires no conditions.

'Conditional self-esteem' that fluctuates based on external circumstances, along with all elements that teach, instill, and trigger it, constitutes humanity's greatest adversary. And confident self-esteem that exists regardless of conditions is the healthy 'self-identity' that everyone should strive to find. Not something newly created, but what has always been inherently present.

To emphasize again, identity should not be 'conditional content' but rather 'cognitive self-awareness of the imperative of unconditional wholeness' and 'the solid and confident feeling based on this awareness.' Conditions and content merely provide supplementary support to this foundation. Willingly embracing and utilizing all aspects of myself while existing confidently and naturally regardless of them, whether content exists or not, even setting aside all content—this is the feeling of 'being,' the authentic sense of existence. This is precisely the most fundamental identity and existentiality.

This is not something newly created or added. It is already, originally, and always as it is. However, we have been under an illusion, trapped in a strange pattern of treating the accumulated contents of our lives as conditions for our identity and existential value. Since we have lived in that illusion for a long time, and society and culture reinforce it, to break free from this misconception, we need to intentionally redirect our mind's eye to vividly experience our original identity. Once you become clearly aware of this, you will naturally begin to experience its benefits.

- Identity is not who I am; rather, I am the owner of my identity

One incorrect belief we typically take for granted is the unconscious notion that 'existence requires justification.' It is a peculiar belief that to be recognized as a person, one must satisfy certain reasons and conditions. Most of us accept this belief unconditionally and uncritically. However, no such requirement exists. Our existence needs no justification. Attempting to find the reason or justification for existence within the content of life becomes an endless game, a problem without solution. This is because these 'contents' are constructs imposed upon me by myself, others, and the world.

The very fact that you exist now is evidence that all reasons and conditions for existence have already been fulfilled. If the conditions and reasons were insufficient, neither you nor I would have existed in the first place. One must reclaim this feeling of 'unconditional solidity and confidence' in the inner self that emerges from the self-awareness of this truth. A sense of existence that we possessed at birth and still retain today, yet has become obscured by strange conditions and rules imposed by the world, others, and ourselves.

There is no need to wander in search of a more impressive, complete, energetic, or mature version of ourselves. We need only

to clearly recognize and gradually erase all these 'not-me selves'—
all the 'negative, passive selves' that the world, others, and we
ourselves have layered upon our being since birth—understanding
that they are merely temporary constructs, groundless limitations,
and awkward restrictions. We can simply let them go. We can
simply disregard them. It follows the same principle as when light
appears and shadows naturally vanish. Nothing can constrain me
unless I, the master of myself, allow it. One must firmly maintain
this mindset because it is fundamentally true. Then, in the space
where the 'not-me selves' have fallen away, let us sincerely feel,
embrace, and accept the authentic self that has always been present.
Expressed in words, it is this:

"Just as I am now, I am already enough."
"Just as I am now, I am already worthy."
"I am already proud of myself just as I am right now."
"I am already lovable just as I am right now."

We can perceive the identity of others in this way as well. For
instance, the best healing that parents can offer their children
comes through words such as these:

"I support and love you just as you are, regardless of what you
do."
"While I would be proud of your successes and achievements, I
am proud of you regardless—even without them."
"Whatever choice you make, I will support you."

Because that is its inherent nature. This is not a matter of belief
but rather one of awareness and perception. Whether in family,
school, or society, providing children with such healthy sense of self

and identity should be the primary goal. The 'content' is merely a supplementary tool. For instance, utilizing an individual's unique characteristics, strengths, and aspects—the 'content'—to healthily establish their uniqueness and identity and to elevate their self-esteem, self-respect, satisfaction, and self-confidence is a reasonably effective approach. So if one can establish a strong and healthy existence as an individual from the beginning and form relationships with the world to live happily, what could be wrong with that?

Nevertheless, what is constructed in this way is not a true identity but rather should be called 'individuality' or 'individual nature' in a narrower sense. The strategy of attempting to make such individuality or individual nature one's unique identity and existential value has fundamental limitations and may potentially produce adverse effects. This is because it relies on elements that are highly volatile and temporary in nature. No matter how much we attempt to expand it, individuality determined by content inherently cannot escape the fate of being 'limited' or 'restricted'. Whether to accept this reality remains within the realm of free choice, but failing to recognize it leads us to believe this limitation constitutes the entirety of our identity, leaving no room for alternatives.

Identity transcends 'concepts, knowledge, constructs, and discernment'—it exists beyond such classifications. Therefore, if there exists one unique foundation that each individual can claim as their true identity, it is precisely this 'unbounded identity'. Existing so boldly and vividly in this moment, while simultaneously refusing to be constrained by any limitation. 'Unbounded' is synonymous with 'unlimited,' which essentially means 'infinite.' It is an infinity that transcends and exists independently of the conceptual frame of finitude and infinitude. Thus, it is an infinity that moves with remarkable lightness.

Does this imply 'an absence of identity'? Certainly not. It means that my identity is not me, but rather I am the owner of that identity. I am a being that embraces all identities while simultaneously transcending them. With a clear foundation of 'unbounded identity' or from a position beyond all identities, one freely and comfortably utilizes whatever identity is needed in the moment and then releases it.

There is a fundamental difference between utilizing conditions from a state of having realized the 'unconditional necessity of existence' versus utilizing conditions while trapped in the premise that 'existence inherently requires certain conditions.' For example, let's consider two individuals who share similar social circumstances and engage in comparable activities. One person does not base their existence and sense of legitimacy on their actions and conditions, while the other still depends on these conditions; these two individuals are living entirely different lives. It is essential to recognize this distinction.

Our existence requires no conditions.
Conditions are merely tools to be utilized as needed.
Without relying on any internally accumulated memories,
Without relying on any externally accumulated achievements or unfulfilled goals
We can exist as our complete, authentic selves.
And we simply need to fulfill what must be done.

Summary

Identity is not content but a feeling. True identity emerges from unconditional self-esteem and a firm sense of self. Our existence requires neither reason nor condition. We are already sufficient as we are, and we remain valuable beings regardless of our actions or achievements. Identity is unlimited, and we are the masters of our own identity. Conditions are merely tools to be used according to necessity.

3.2 Will you become an existence living according to the scenario, or will you become the subject who creates the scenario?

: Breaking Free from Negative Scenarios Imposed by Parents and Society in the Past

The psychological problems we encounter in life can be broadly categorized into two types: emotional disorders and cognitive impairments. Emotional disorders occur when the emotional aftermath of unpleasant, sad, or traumatic past experiences remains imprinted in our minds, periodically resurfacing in daily life and exerting negative influences. At this point, the experience manifests not only emotionally but can also be physically perceived through the five senses.

While emotional disorders pertain to 'disturbances in emotion,' cognitive impairments represent 'disorders of thought' or 'disruptions in understanding.' These may arise purely from cognitive errors themselves, but more frequently they accompany the emotional and sensory traumas previously discussed. Simply put, it is suffering caused by 'distorted thinking.' Is it not common that even when our thoughts are flawed, we struggle to view them objectively or make corrections? The reason is that we do not view thoughts as 'merely thoughts' but instead identify them with our 'self.'

Here, I will explore cognitive impairment through the concept of 'scenario dysfunction.' In essence, it is a dysfunction that occurs due to 'incorrect scenarios' about human relationships and how the world operates. Scenario dysfunction is also a concept used in some established psychological frameworks, and it typically begins around ages 7-11, corresponding to elementary school years in

Korean society (though it can certainly develop later as well). What are the most significant changes that occur in children (ourselves) during this developmental period?

The first is 'linguistic influence'. From this period onward, one becomes governed by scripts—the 'linguistic rules' that define one's behavior and social roles. Unlike earlier stages when linguistic activity lacked sophistication, during this period the influence of language becomes highly 'concrete' and 'operational,' enabling operational thinking according to various rule systems. A prime example is the newfound ability to comprehend various mathematical concepts and social rules.

Another significant change occurs when one becomes capable of viewing the world from 'others' perspectives' and assuming different roles. Until this point, conscious attention that was solely focused inward begins to extend outward. That is, as one begins to observe others and the world, one becomes integrated into society, which operates according to regular or established scenarios.

Through encountering and internalizing 'external scenarios,' one begins to create personal frameworks for understanding the world. In essence, one develops an individualized comprehension of reality. Well-constructed scenarios prove extremely valuable. When scenarios are already properly understood, one can respond more easily and build relationships with people more efficiently.

The problem arises when scenarios are incorrectly constructed or improperly utilized. This can be collectively referred to as 'scenario dysfunction'.

- Negative myths imposed from external sources

During our elementary school years, the scenarios we internalize come from our parents and society. Not all of these narratives represent absolute truth. In essence, they are merely 'myths' belonging exclusively to parents or the external world. Those scenarios were merely created by them, just as I would create my own.

Children who lack the ability to judge and modify uncritically accept all these scenarios. And although it is merely a single myth or scenario, we accept it as 'absolute fact or truth.' As we age and gain experience, our personal judgment and power of thought increase, allowing us to modify, discard, or develop previously accepted scenarios; however, not infrequently, they solidify as 'my absolute scenarios.'

And when what we believed to be 'accurate facts about the world' turns out to be the 'incorrect scenario' created by parents, certain individuals, or society, we experience greater suffering, especially as the degree of distortion and error increases.

Children who grew up receiving significant negative influence from their parents are the most common example. Through the parents' incorrect scenarios, the child is continuously instilled with self-images such as 'incompetent child, bad child, insufficient child, lazy child, child who should not have been born, child who will never amount to anything.' One continues to receive negative reactions about one's own behaviors. One is continuously fed distorted interpretations and perspectives about the world.

The child will sometimes conform and sometimes rebel, but in either case, these scenarios infiltrate the child's consciousness and become essentially 'learned.' This occurs because of the uncritical nature mentioned earlier. It happens because the child lacks the conscious strength to resist it. It happens because this is a time when one must simply accept. Even a child who dislikes the scenario presented by parents unknowingly begins to believe in that scenario. What a painful situation this is. Despite consciously disliking and rejecting it, one becomes unknowingly occupied and entangled by it. It is a kind of paradoxical situation.

Not only parents but also teachers, surrounding adults, and peers can play such negative roles. Usually, it's long-term or intense stimuli that persist, but sometimes a fragment of a negative scenario casually thrown at our younger selves in passing can dominate our minds for a lifetime. Haven't you experienced this yourself?

Not only individuals but also society and culture play a role in instilling negative and distorted scenarios. These may manifest as collective or social customs, religious doctrines, or specific modes of thinking characteristic of a particular era and region. All forms of prejudice, discrimination, aversion, and irrational or unreasonable customs that exist within a society fall into this category. For instance, Korean society harbors its own collective error scenarios. Notable examples include the culture obsessed with age hierarchy, the military culture pervasive throughout society, persistent gender-based discrimination, excessive interference in individual lives, and discriminatory attitudes toward social minorities such as people with disabilities and sexual minorities. These issues, of course, are not unique to Korean society. Every society, according to its level of development, encompasses various immature and mature scenarios in its own unique way.

- Negative Myths We Create Ourselves

Based on scenarios we have uncritically accepted, we now create our own pathological narratives. This includes all the negative or error-laden self-images, worldviews, value systems, and situational judgments that we, as adults who have grown from children, 'ourselves' now hold. It began as something absorbed from the external world, but at some point, it transformed into something we identify as 'mine.'

If my scenario seems incorrect, I can simply fix it or discard it.   In reality, we often find ourselves unable to discard our scenarios, instead stubbornly clinging to them. There are two primary reasons for this. One is the belief that 'my scenario must be correct because I created it with my best effort.' Another reason is the concept of identification where 'my scenario is myself.' In other words, denying the scenario is perceived as denying oneself, leading to the error of protecting an incorrect scenario in an attempt to preserve one's sense of self. Even though in reality it doesn't protect me but rather causes me harm.

For example, there are individuals who view themselves or the world exclusively through a negative lens. When such a person is suffering and struggling, friends or acquaintances might try to offer supportive words: "You're a good person. "You're a wonderful person" or "This situation is actually fine for these reasons" - they attempt to present a more positive scenario, but the individual rejects and denies these perspectives.

While this seems irrational from a common sense perspective, understanding the underlying psychological mechanism makes it comprehensible. In other words, it is a negative scenario that torments you, but because it has already become 'your scenario,' you identify yourself with it. Furthermore, because you believe this scenario is 'correct,' you cling to it and stubbornly maintain it. It's not actually correct but merely 'familiar,' yet due to the erroneous belief that 'what is familiar must be right,' you perceive it as truth.

Because humans must navigate the world based on some form of personal narrative, we require scenarios—whether beneficial or harmful—to make sense of our existence. Therefore, unless we change to a different scenario, we have no choice but to continue relying on the existing one. That is, we view ourselves and the world according to the existing scenario not because the scenario is accurate or beneficial, but because we need some scenario regardless.

However, essentially, we can exist without any problems whether a specific scenario is present or not. In other words, scenarios are merely tools; they do not determine our existentiality.

- The scenario is not 'me'

The scenario dysfunction in the pathological conditions we have examined thus far is not fundamentally different from the scenario dysfunction that occurs in everyday life. The difference lies in the 'degree' of severity. That is, if the degree of transformation, error, or illusion exceeds a certain threshold, it becomes a pathological disorder; otherwise, it remains merely a minor everyday impediment. Even in the absence of pathology, we frequently encounter difficulties. These include our minor errors, small conflicts between spouses, family members, or colleagues, and slight misalignments experienced in social interactions. After all, no perfect scenario exists. Rather, recognizing and acknowledging our errors is the secret to living a more flexible and enriched life.

However, when errors are too significant, they can cause profound self-torment, necessitating solutions. By clinging to incorrect scenarios, we may gain immediate psychological stability and satisfaction, but ultimately suffer pain and loss as relationships and situations become increasingly difficult and inefficient. Therefore, for our own benefit—not for anyone else's—we must resolve issues arising from incorrect scenarios as thoroughly as possible. What thoughts and methods can help? The answer lies in synthesizing the principles we have already discussed.

First, a scenario is merely a scenario. It is not an 'absolute truth.' Nor does this mean it's 'fiction.' There is no need to debate whether it's fact or fiction. It is sufficient to recognize that a scenario is simply a scenario. A scenario is a tool that we create and utilize to live our lives more purposefully and efficiently. Our task is not whether to create scenarios, but rather to 'create them well and use them effectively.' The 'self' is not an existence that lives according to scenarios. I am the subject who creates and modifies these scenarios.

Second, do not identify yourself with the scenario. My scenario about the world is my unique 'interpretation' of my relationships with others and how the world functions. Just because I created and possess this scenario doesn't mean that it constitutes 'me'. We are not insignificant beings limited or restricted by mere scenarios. We are beings who contain them while existing beyond them. To identify oneself with a scenario is comparable to equating the entire world with a single book. It is inefficient and foolish. Acknowledge scenarios for what they are, but do not identify yourself with them. Do not regard them as 'all-encompassing' or 'absolute.'

Third, distinguish the external mythical scenarios that have been implanted within you. If it's a scenario I've created within myself, it may be worthy of some respect. I try not to absolutize even my own scenarios, let alone those implanted from outside. Aren't those merely 'their myths'? Why should I be swayed by and trapped in others' myths? There is no necessity for this. Let them live confined in their myths—that is their portion. What about me? I don't need to participate in unnecessary myths and scenarios created by others and the world. Of course, as we engage in social life and form relationships, there are times when we inevitably respond to or become involved in the absurd scenarios created by others and society. Even if I outwardly comply to a certain extent, I need not completely acknowledge or accept these scenarios in my heart.

Fourth, let's steadily discard what needs to be discarded and modify what needs to be modified, not just in others' scenarios but also in our own mythical narratives. For our own well-being. The original initial scenario was also created in that manner. Just because something was created first does not make it more absolute, more accurate, or more important. It was simply created 'at the beginning, in the early stages.' Do we consider someone more precious and more important than others simply because we met them first? No, that's absurd. The same applies to scenarios.

Beyond this approach, there are many other methods to resolve the scenario problems associated with pathological conditions. Through our individual wisdom, we can create numerous different and better solutions. Let us employ these methods as well. What could possibly prevent us? There are no limitations. In doing so, let us utilize and continuously develop more flexible and mature life scenarios. The essential focus remains 'my own happiness'. Moreover, when I create and implement more accurate, precise, and mature scenarios, both others and the world naturally become happier as a result.

◆ ◆ ◆

Summary

We are influenced by negative scenarios we receive from our parents and society during childhood. These scenarios shape our self-image and worldview, but they are not necessarily true. Scenarios are merely tools and do not define our existence. For a healthy life, we must recognize these scenarios, avoid identifying ourselves with them, and know when to modify or discard them as needed. As creators and masters of our scenarios, we can develop more flexible and mature life narratives.

3.3 Why do we need recognition from others and the world?

: Breaking Free from External Evaluation

We humans not only feel our own inadequacies but also continuously experience pride and self-satisfaction. In most cases, feelings of inadequacy overshadow or offset satisfaction, but on the other hand, there is a feeling of 'Still, I did my best. I did what I had to do in my own way. I'm doing well in my own right.' 'I want that to be recognized!' This sentiment exists within us. This is not a flawed or weak mindset, but rather a completely natural and healthy psychological response. As long as it does not devolve into arrogance, coercion, or excessive desire, this becomes the foundation for genuine pride and healthy self-esteem.

While it would be beneficial to acknowledge oneself by affirming 'I did well, I am okay,' many individuals find this self-validation insufficient and seek confirmation from others. They desire recognition. This, too, is a natural and healthy psychological need, as the self and others are not entirely separate entities.

There is a hidden structure here as well. The fundamental reason we seek validation from others is ultimately to validate ourselves through it. It becomes a means for self-acceptance.

You can understand the psychological mechanism at work here. However, it is highly inefficient. This is because one must receive validation from others to feel satisfied and able to accept oneself. We cannot always receive recognition from others, and it's like taking an unnecessary detour when a direct path exists. The outcome of receiving self-acceptance through external validation and simply granting yourself self-acceptance directly is ultimately the same. Above all, who exactly are these 'others and the world' that we so absolutely depend on and seek validation from? Are they gods or absolute beings? No. They are simply existences exactly like ourselves.

Let us give others and the world only the roles that are appropriate for them—within the context of mutual love and respect, of course. That is sufficient. There is no need to grant them excessive power. What we must focus on is the original purpose: self-acceptance.

This mental habit of 'only feeling validated when receiving recognition from external sources and others' must eventually be overcome. It means directly embracing the original purpose of 'self-acceptance'. However, it must be 'unconditional self-acceptance' rather than 'conditional self-acceptance'.

When the external world and others recognize you first, willingly accept and enjoy that recognition. And whenever you need their recognition, you may freely create situations worthy of receiving it. Allow yourself this freedom. Furthermore, if there are conditions that others or I require, I can create, achieve, and embody them.

Above all, even without such conditions, I can simply live as myself—always doing my best, feeling satisfied, maintaining confidence, and living naturally. With this expanded energy and mindset, one can live more confidently and admirably in everyday life.

◆ ◆ ◆

Summary

We often seek self-acceptance through the validation of others. However, this is an inefficient and circuitous approach. Instead, it is important to actively practice unconditional self-acceptance. Accept validation from others, but do not become entirely dependent on it. We can acknowledge our worth and live confidently regardless of external circumstances. This self-acceptance leads to a more abundant and confident life.

3.4 What we truly fear is not 'decision' but 'experience'

: Cultivating the Courage to Make Decisive Choices

I encounter surprisingly many people who worry, 'Could I have decision paralysis?' It's problematic to use the term 'disability' carelessly, and in reality, rather than being a true 'disability,' it's often merely a difficulty in making decisions, yet it's inappropriately labeled as such.

Everyone finds decision-making difficult. It's merely a matter of degree. After making difficult decisions, we experience anxiety. Why do we struggle with this fundamental aspect of choice? If we understand the root causes, we can transform ourselves to approach moments of decision with greater composure and flexibility.

- Is there a predetermined answer or a correct choice?

The primary reason we hesitate at the moment of decision-making is our belief that 'somewhere out there exists the perfect choice or optimal decision.' There may indeed be matters where a predetermined or optimal answer exists. If an optimal choice exists, one should naturally seek and explore it. Business decisions or important choices should never be made carelessly. One should make choices by investing one's best analysis, careful consideration, relevant data, and personal insight. This is especially true in cases that entail significant responsibility or consequences. Deliberating before such decisions is not what is colloquially called 'decision paralysis,' but rather a natural cautiousness.

When we wonder, 'Why can't I make decisions?' it's usually not about significant choices but rather our inability to make everyday decisions. Therefore, we must first address decision-making situations in our daily lives. If 'decision-making' skills are first developed in this area, they can later be applied when facing truly important decisions.

Whether in serious circumstances or everyday situations, ultimately the necessity of choosing among several options remains the same. Sometimes the timing of a decision is more important than the decision itself. Yet what if you hesitate ambivalently and miss the crucial moment of decision? Being trained to make decisions at appropriate times is far more important than one might think. This is, in fact, the primary purpose of writing this text.

We must first shatter the illusion that 'there is a predetermined answer, correct choice, or optimal decision for everything.' It's not that you shouldn't seek such beliefs, but rather that you shouldn't let unnecessary and excessive preoccupation with them interfere with your choices and decisions. There are three new mental frames we should adopt while searching for the best options.

1. What I choose becomes the answer.
2. I am the one creating the answer.
3. The answer is not necessarily fixed as just one option.

The first frame, 'What I choose becomes the answer,' is one of the most powerful solutions. No one would interpret this statement to mean that decisions can be made carelessly. It means to strive to make the optimal decision with your utmost effort, but when the time comes to decide, stop hesitating or faltering and proceed with the mindset that 'what I have chosen is the answer.' And in reality, this is indeed the case.

At every moment of decision, our minds are subtly undermined by the thought, 'What if my choice is not the optimal or best option?' This is why we become anxious and hesitate. However, no one knows which among options A, B, or C would be the optimal choice until observing the actual process and results. Many people select A and then anxiously wonder, 'Perhaps it should have been B or C?' and if they choose B, they worry, 'Perhaps it should have been A or C?'

Strictly speaking, the burden of anxiety remains identical regardless of which option you select. 'What if what I've chosen isn't the right answer?' they ponder. Therefore, given the equivalent emotional cost, it is more effective and beneficial to simply adopt the perspective that 'What I have chosen is indeed the answer.' It is useful in the moment of choice and empowers the subsequent journey. Therefore, there is no reason not to abandon the frame of hesitation and adopt the frame of determination.

Second, the principle that 'I am the one creating the answer' follows the same logic. If you reach a situation where you can no longer distinguish which option is superior, or where any choice causes hesitation, strictly speaking, only the task of 'creating your own answer' remains. Yet as long as you continue to vaguely believe that 'there exists an inherent right answer,' and therefore think 'I must select it correctly,' you cannot stand firmly in the face of decisions. Unless it's a truly exceptional case, there's no such thing. I'm simply creating the answer myself. That is the reality.

'How can someone like me create answers?' You might think, 'Isn't that something only special, perfect people can do?' There are no separate special people. No, I am that special person. There are no predetermined qualifications or conditions that determine who is entitled to create answers in the first place. Let's intentionally adopt the mindset that 'I am precisely the person who can create answers.'

Even if it feels awkward at first, let's continue to repeat, establish, and strengthen these practices. Then, at some point, you will actually become such a person and naturally act in that way. Of course, this happens while steadily building up the appropriate conditions, qualifications, and capabilities.

Third, it's important to remember that 'The answer is not necessarily limited to one.' There can be multiple answers. We select one among them based on our needs. Therefore, what you choose becomes the answer, and in this way, you become the creator of your own answers. I reiterate, let us never cease in our efforts to make the most appropriate and suitable decisions for each situation. However, amidst this consideration, when the moment truly calls for a decision, we must act decisively. The mindset that 'the answer is not necessarily singular or fixed' is a frame that helps us make decisions more comfortably and flexibly when needed. We should utilize this approach actively.

As previously discussed, one of the primary psychological factors that causes hesitation in decision-making is our 'lingering attachment to the options we did not choose.' The feeling that 'If I had chosen that instead of this, it would have been better.' However, this is merely an illusion. It is the continued pursuit of a dream that will never be fulfilled. Once you have decided on one option from among many, the others essentially become 'non-existent.' Continuing to desire what no longer exists is an illusion and only depletes your mental energy. This is not to say you should disregard or ignore alternative options. Rather, it means releasing unnecessary attachments that do not contribute to the progress of your work.

Any decision inevitably carries its own advantages and disadvantages in both process and outcome. Naturally, we strive to make decisions that minimize drawbacks while maximizing benefits. Therefore, in business or important matters, we must exert our utmost effort to make appropriate decisions. Nevertheless, whether facing everyday choices or significant decisions, we ultimately confront the reality that 'choosing one option means lacking something else, and choosing the alternative means missing the first.'

Let us consider the opposite perspective instead. We can intentionally focus on the abundance each choice brings: 'choosing this enriches one aspect of life, while choosing that enhances another.' This is not about pretending to be unaware of or ignoring the areas where you are lacking or insufficient. Even after making a decision, if there are aspects I need to supplement or modify, I can certainly do so. However, it is about the 'mind frame' with which you approach the situation. If a decision cannot be reversed, it is clearly wise to find and enjoy the best in what you have already chosen. This holds true psychologically as well.

- Whatever decision you make, the subsequent process remains the same

Making choices and decisions is certainly not everything. Rather, the decision is merely the beginning. After deciding, you go through a process. And now we must face the truth: we are not afraid of making decisions. In other words, we don't suffer from 'decision paralysis'. What we truly fear is the process that follows after making a decision.

We constantly dream of 'a better process after a good decision, a more comfortable journey ahead.' However, regardless of what decision we make, the 'post-decision process' remains fundamentally the same. This doesn't mean that all content and progression are identical, but rather that the overall experiential journey follows similar patterns. The differences aren't so fundamental as to justify hesitating, postponing, or avoiding decisions altogether. It is a distinction that allows one to be sufficiently detached if one simply decides to be. Therefore, it is best to consider from the outset that 'all processes following the decision are identical.'

The most powerful method is precisely 'willingly experiencing.'

In other words, whether it's the process after choosing A or choosing B or C, it's about 'willingly experiencing everything' without making significant distinctions. This is certainly not easy. However, it's not impossible either. There are no alternatives. What purpose is there in saying 'I don't want to experience this!' after making a decision? Hesitating about the experience is equally pointless. Postponing or hesitating over choices and decisions yields no particular benefit; rather, it often leads to unnecessary difficulties or losses that could have been avoided. So why deliberately avoid 'making the necessary decision in the moment'?

The mindsets beneficial to adopt when experiencing the aftermath of a decision are as follows. Initially, anxiety and fear arise precisely from the absence of the mindsets described below.

First, do not regret your decisions. Proper reflection and analysis are certainly valuable. However, regret is worse than its absence. Reflection or analysis brings desirable changes to the process after a decision, but regret only produces negative emotions without productive change and merely drains energy.

Second, even after making a decision, continue to carefully observe the process and results. This is not due to anxiety or lack of self-confidence. By continuing to examine the process, you complete the decision you've made. This strengthens your capacity for future decisions as well.

Third, when correction or redirection is needed, commit to it wholeheartedly. This isn't about regretting or dismissing your original decision. No matter how confident we are in a decision, the subsequent process continues to evolve and cannot be permanently fixed. Such certainty is impossible. Therefore, we should not hesitate to make appropriate adjustments and transitions after making a decision.

Fourth, there remains something we must not forget. Unless truly exceptional circumstances arise that require reversing or halting our original decision, we should 'maintain our initial decision until the end.' This doesn't mean irrationally clinging to previous decisions or being unreasonably stubborn. Rather, it means strengthening our resolve. This is because repeatedly reversing decisions too easily, giving up, or stopping can unintentionally weaken trust in your own decisions and diminish self-confidence. Moreover, others' trust in you becomes undermined. While it takes courage to change when change is truly necessary, it requires equal courage to remain steadfast when change is not warranted.

'Maintaining a decision until the end' is a form of conscious training. This mindset serves as a foundation that helps you make decisions with maximum deliberation, continue giving your best throughout the process, and willingly embrace whatever results may come.

This is also about 'courage'. In other words, 'willingly experiencing' is another term for 'the courage to face life's experiences with dignity'. The key insight is that moments of decision continue to pass us by whether we exercise courage or not, and making appropriate decisions in those moments ultimately benefits us the most.

To have the courage to willingly decide and willingly experience, one must trust oneself and the overall flow of circumstances. There are numerous instances where we hesitate to make decisions due to a lack of self-trust. In such situations, we should ask ourselves: 'Have I prepared for this decision diligently and rationally enough?' 'Will I continue to do my best after making the decision?'

If you can answer 'yes' to these questions, don't hesitate—trust yourself. This means intentionally choosing to believe in your capabilities. Additionally, develop trust in the natural flow of circumstances. Trusting in circumstances is somewhat different from trusting in oneself. I'm not suggesting that you believe in concepts like luck or fate. If I am doing my absolute best, then I can intentionally trust that the greater situation—which I cannot fully comprehend—will unfold favorably. This approach brings significantly more stability to the mind.

You will naturally worry and feel anxious about whether you have prepared adequately, and whether your decision will allow the situation to progress appropriately. This is where you must exercise the aforementioned skill of 'recognizing and transcending illusions'—specifically, the illusion that there exists one optimal choice. If I am certain that I will continue to do my best both before and after making a decision, I should trust myself and the situation. With this trust as a foundation, I must continue to give my best effort.

◆ ◆ ◆

Summary

The difficulty of decision-making stems from the illusion of 'the optimal choice.' In reality, what we choose becomes the answer, and we ourselves create that answer. We tend to fear the experiences that follow a decision rather than the decision itself. However, regardless of which choice we make, the subsequent process is often similar. What's important is willingly experiencing the process after making a decision, not regretting it, and maintaining the decision until the end while making necessary adjustments. The key is to make decisions with courage while trusting yourself and the situation.

3.5 We need not rush to be 'ultimately right'

: Overcoming the Impatience of 'I Must Be Right'

There is a story of a Korean exchange professor that I read in a newspaper column long ago. It was approximately the following account.

As an exchange professor in the United States, he was assigned to teach one class. His students were undergraduates. It was a course where students would take turns expressing their thoughts and proposing solutions to social problems that had been assigned a week in advance, followed by discussion. Since these were topics for which standard analyses and solutions were already established, the professor anticipated that students would conduct their presentations and discussions with relative ease.

Astonishingly, the presentations were uniformly inadequate and disappointing, leading him to question whether these were truly university students. Korean students would have researched and organized various materials in advance to deliver polished presentations, but the American students had not managed to do this. As the professor observed them presenting and discussing inconsequential content well past the midpoint of the class, they grew increasingly bored and considered, 'Perhaps I should simply provide the answer myself.'

As the class progressed into its final stages, a remarkable transformation began to unfold. The seemingly disorganized content gradually began to coalesce. Ultimately, they arrived at an excellent conclusion. It was a conclusion that would have been difficult to reach had I merely referenced existing materials. Upon reflection, I realized that students weren't passive during seemingly 'trivial' presentations. They were sharing their thoughts with one another, reconstructing their own ideas based on this exchange, then presenting these refined concepts—a continuous process of distillation until they reached the essential understanding.

In such situations, Korean students typically seek out existing content and predetermined answers from external sources for their presentations. The content is excellent, but it is not self-created. If the topic were to suddenly change, one would not be able to produce similar results through their own efforts. In contrast, American students, although they initially started at a level where they barely understood the fundamentals, did their best to express their thoughts and knew how to absorb and utilize others' ideas as their own. This included even content they were unfamiliar with or that contradicted their own perspectives.

In other words, to develop thoughts and arrive at answers, they knew how to utilize not only their own resources but also those of others. Not hastening to assert one's correctness or knowledge, but understanding—both intellectually and viscerally—that drawing proper conclusions through efficient methods benefits both oneself and others.

Why are we so quick to establish the 'single correct answer' and to position ourselves as the 'answer holder'?

The correct answer is never static. It continuously evolves according to circumstances. In this sense, the correct answer is not something predetermined but always in motion, representing 'what is most appropriate and optimal in this present moment.' The process of determining what is most appropriate and optimal in the present moment is the process of finding the correct answer.

There are primarily two situations in which one seeks the correct answer. One is when you must find the precise answer within a designated timeframe. In such cases, you naturally need to identify the best possible answer under the given conditions. Speed and timing are paramount. The other is finding the optimal answer without significant time constraints. This scenario is more common in everyday life. Of course, this doesn't mean the process can be indefinitely prolonged, but what matters in this case is the 'content' of the answer, not the 'speed'.

The problem clearly arises when we are too hasty or compulsively try to state 'the ultimately correct answer,' even in the second case. But in reality, rather than 'finding the right answer,' we want to assert 'I am right' as quickly and forcefully as possible. We constantly desire to become 'quick answer-givers.'

Three distinct desires are intermingled here. The desire to speak 'quickly,' the urge to assert being 'right,' and finally, the need to emphasize 'myself.' The subject and object have become reversed. The original goal that should have been pursued has disappeared, and something irrelevant has taken its place. This is not a problem limited to authoritarian decision-makers or a select few individuals. It is a common issue for all of us who belong to this society—the attitude that says, 'I am fine, but you are the problem. You need to change your attitude.'

The development of social media has made it easier to observe this phenomenon. Consider several social issues that have recently become heated topics online. There are cultural issues as well as matters related to public figures. Some are political and economic issues, others would have been religious matters, and there would have been historical and ethical concerns as well.

Let us reflect on how hastily I or our society have attempted to arrive at 'definitive correct answers' regarding these issues. The same applies to personal matters that only involve me and my acquaintances. The identical phenomenon manifests, merely differing in magnitude. All misunderstandings and hasty judgments on social media, in the workplace, at school, in various communities, and at home; the rumors and prejudices that form; and the mutual distrust and trauma that inevitably follow...

As illustrated by the exchange professor's experience mentioned at the beginning of the text, what we need is to listen to as many perspectives as possible, understand the situation thoroughly, gather comprehensive data and information, and based on these elements, arrive at the most appropriate 'conclusion, answer, judgment, or choice'. Approaching situations this way is ultimately most advantageous and beneficial to oneself. We need not ask which is more efficient and appropriate: an answer based on minimal information and perspectives, or one based on comprehensive information and multiple viewpoints.

What do we typically do? We tend to rush toward conclusions based solely on what we know 'in the moment.' Despite knowing very little, we formulate 'definitive answers' based on our initial impressions or preliminary assumptions. We feel somehow deficient or problematic if we cannot immediately determine who is right or wrong, what is correct or incorrect. When gathering more information and seeking different opinions, I somehow feel inadequate. I think the same about others. I feel that I cannot make decisions quickly or find the correct answer because something is lacking within me. This stems from the social conditioning I've internalized over time. It is the result of a distorted culture. It's not because it's the right or beneficial method, but because that approach has become familiar to both body and mind. However, we must exercise caution. What is familiar is not necessarily right.

The greater issue is that later, even when examining compiled arguments and evidence, I tend to only notice what aligns with the perspective I had already anticipated. Other arguments or opposing opinions are intentionally or unintentionally ignored. Even when seen, they are treated as if unseen. It is the inability to perceive and accept content and materials as they truly are. Consequently, existing answers remain unchanged. The process by which my established 'rightness' might be transformed by new information does not occur. I have already predetermined the 'final answer.' The subsequent process of gathering information becomes merely a formality.

This is not the case. Not rushing to determine a final answer is not because one is 'lacking, insufficient, or ignorant.' To arrive at appropriate and beneficial answers, everyone needs sufficient information and time for contemplation. No one can produce the right answer without these elements. And except in special cases where quick decisions are necessary, the time and effort invested are never wasted. The results I obtain are beneficial and useful in proportion to what I invest.

- How to Find the Most Beneficial Right Answer

For several decades after the war(戰後), our society needed quick answers and those who could provide them. This was considered a form of unity and capability. Finding, asserting, and implementing the most appropriate and effective solutions within given time constraints. This approach enabled remarkably rapid development.

The influence of distorted Confucian culture and dysfunctional military culture was substantial. The same applies to the imbalanced patriarchal culture. In such cases, the issue lies not in 'speed' but in a culture that disregards diversity and consideration, along with the excessive deference given to 'decision-makers' authority. In other words, decisions were immediately obeyed and uniformly implemented not because they were the most appropriate or effective, but simply because they came from socially sanctioned 'decision-makers.' Even in cases where the decision-maker lacks sufficient ability.

In this culture, the process of determining the correct answer had to be decidedly authoritarian and assertive. I or my group had to produce and assert answers as quickly as possible. We neither listened to nor considered the content, materials, or answers provided by others. There was no time for that, and no mental space. It wasn't that kind of consciousness, that kind of culture. Therefore, we never learned to willingly listen to alternative perspectives and answers, internalize them, and develop more complete solutions—whether individually or collectively. All of us were guilty of this.

In the past, things were much simpler than they are now, and there weren't as many competitors. It was culturally acceptable. Above all, it was familiar. Quick decisions and coordinated actions were undeniably efficient.

But the world has changed.

Every sector of our society has become incredibly complex, and there are more competitors in the international community. Some countries have even surpassed us. Consequently, the 'old ways' no longer work.

Even beyond this, there are clear reasons why we must break free from distorted Confucian culture, military culture, and patriarchal systems. Such cultures ultimately cause suffering to both self and other, to all of us collectively. In short, they were cultures of psychological immaturity. If it had been possible, we should have established a more mature and efficient culture of 'creating constructive solutions' from the very beginning. This isn't necessary merely because times have changed, but because it should have been this way from the outset.

First, let us suspend our attachment to the concept of 'ultimate correctness.' Let's not rush to establish the 'final answer' too quickly, but instead allow ourselves space for reflection.

To do this, I must carefully observe my existing methods and processes for determining what is 'correct and true.' I need to examine whether there are flaws in my approach. These flaws include: attempting to determine the answer 'too hastily,' and strongly believing and wanting to assert that 'I already know the answer.' In essence, it's making the assertion 'I am already right' the ultimate goal. Even if we don't express this outwardly, internally we crave this self-affirming sensation. The psychological tendency to want to believe 'I already know the right answer.' Without this belief, one experiences a sense of unease.

All of this ultimately connects to the error of attempting to assert one's self. This is not to say that self-assertion is inherently wrong. It means we need 'the most efficient and accurate answer' and should focus on that, as it constitutes our original purpose. And 'the error of mistaking the familiar for the correct' is another aspect that warrants careful examination.

Our goal is to find 'the best opinion, thought, and correct answer,' not to assert that 'I and my claims are unconditionally right.' We must not confuse these two positions. Let us become aware of our pattern of identifying our thoughts, opinions, and answers with our 'self' and our self-esteem, and our tendency to defend these at all costs. Let us confront the unconscious desire to protect the 'self' in this manner.

When we need to solve actual problems, this desire is not helpful at all. In fact, it more often causes harm than good. Ultimately, it inflicts damage and suffering upon both ourselves and others. What we truly need is not to hastily determine or compete over 'who is right or wrong, correct or incorrect,' nor to quickly demonstrate that 'I am right.' It is about collaboratively developing effective and accurate opinions, thoughts, and solutions that benefit all of us, including both self and other.

Let us refrain from hastily claiming and asserting 'I am right' or insisting on 'absolute correctness.' Let us freely express and communicate what each of us considers 'right' in any given moment. Let us permit our own free expression while equally honoring the free expression of others. As we continue this process of speaking to one another, listening to each other's perspectives, and refining our thoughts, we naturally and gradually find our center. It is about sharing the center that has been established through such a thorough process. Then, a more complete center is newly established. This process continues to elevate and repeat itself.

Nevertheless, let each of us assertively express 'what we believe to be right during the intermediate process' to the best of our ability. This is how we help both ourselves and others. There is no need to think ambiguously or speak hesitantly simply because you are in the middle of the process. If something seems right to you at that moment, at that particular stage, you should express it with clarity. "My best thought and answer at this moment is as follows." This is how the most appropriate center forms at that stage. Urgent matters and tasks requiring prioritization can be handled according to their specific circumstances. Even if it's not the 'ultimate truth or final answer,' let's create and utilize 'situation-specific truths and provisional answers' that are optimal for each circumstance. Let's complete what needs to be done.

Throughout this process, let's always acknowledge that these aren't final solutions. Let's maintain self-awareness that they are neither absolute nor complete. Let's not hastily treat something as all-encompassing or final. By maintaining this perspective, we can continue to discover better answers, more appropriate choices, and improved conclusions. Let us embrace this process together, trusting and believing in one another. This approach benefits both ourselves and everyone around us.

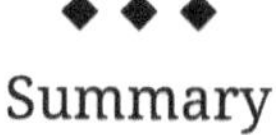

Summary

We must resist the urge to rush toward 'definitive answers.' Instead, we should engage in the process of listening to diverse perspectives, gathering information, and developing a comprehensive understanding of the situation. Rather than clinging to initial judgments, we should cultivate an open attitude toward new information. Rather than hastily asserting 'I am right,' one should focus on finding solutions that benefit everyone. It is important to share one's best thinking at each stage while recognizing that these are not final answers, maintaining an attitude of continually seeking better conclusions.

3.6 There are no bad personalities, only unskilled masters

: Mastering Your Personality Rather Than Being Overwhelmed by It

Many individuals struggle with personality-related issues. Whether one is timid or bold, negative or positive—each temperament brings its own set of concerns. Of course, every personality has its strengths and weaknesses, so no personality is entirely problematic. Inevitably, as we tend to focus more on our shortcomings, we begin to worry about them. If this worry becomes entrenched, it can potentially drain our vital life energy.

While some people live comfortably with their innate personality without particular concerns, even these individuals fall into a universal trap: the 'identification with one's personality.' Thus, at some point, everyone is inevitably constrained by their personality and experiences limitations because of it.

Regarding personality, there is only one solution. We face a choice: to live buried in and suffering from our personality, or to live as the master of our personality, conquering and utilizing it effectively. Our goal is, naturally, the latter.

- Conquering as the master of your personality rather than being buried in it

Opinions are divided on whether personality is innate or formed through environment and developmental processes. Even the most recent neuroscience research suggests approximately a 50-50 distribution between these factors. It is the influence of nurturing and environment upon one's innate foundation. In reality, we have a general understanding of our innate personality and disposition. And while some aspects change as we progress through life, we also recognize that certain parts remain relatively constant, much like our innate skin color.

In some respects, personality may be comparable to how each person is born with different hair, skin color, athletic ability, singing talent, artistic aptitude, and so forth. It is not about being good or bad, superior or inferior, but rather 'simply being different from one another.' If everyone in the world possessed the same dominant personality type, or conversely, if everyone were timid, the Earth would have perished long ago. Therefore, every personality has inherent value in its existence. Each personality plays a role in creating balance and harmony within the whole.

Regardless of whether innate traits or developed characteristics exert more influence, we ultimately develop our own unique personality to some degree. Therefore, rather than merely worrying about your already formed personality, you must conquer it as its master. The difficulty of this task is what makes it problematic.

There are two insights that can help with this process. This can be considered a reorganization of the points mentioned earlier. Let's internalize this knowledge.

First insight: personality is not who you are. It is a life tool that you use.

'I' am a being created through the combination of countless elements. Moreover, I am a being that encompasses all those elements and transcends them, precisely because I contain them all. Past experiences, memories, education, upbringing, appearance, qualifications, abilities, acquaintances, parents, religion, intellect, self-images, evaluations from others and oneself, name, and personality. Even if all these things are combined, they do not constitute 'me'. I cannot be limited or confined by any single element, nor by the sum of all elements. This is because even if some elements are missing, even if all elements were to disappear, I could still exist proudly and confidently as I am. Now, try erasing all of those things. Try to imagine, as if playing a thought experiment, that nothing of your identity remains and you exist solely as the consciousness that perceives everything. How does it feel? It's perfectly fine. Nothing adverse happens.

Since it's imagination, one might object: 'If my past, career, memories, credentials, parents, and knowledge actually disappeared, wouldn't I become nothing? Wouldn't that be catastrophic?' That very worry itself is merely imagination and illusion. An illusion that emerges when you believe these external factors control you and determine your intrinsic value. Of course, if memories, possessions, or the past disappear, one will not become completely identical to how they were before. But here we are referring to 'myself' who exists regardless of any internal or external conditions. That feeling of dignified and honorable existence. This is something that no one and nothing else can affect except myself—unless I eliminate or weaken it myself.

In actual reality, the world constantly tries to define me with 'conditions,' attempts to assign value to me, and tries to impose or strip away meaning from my existence. Even I myself am doing this to me. You might think that others judge you in that way, but it is you who decides whether to accept their judgment, never them. It is I myself who ultimately permits that decision. But many people don't realize this and believe that others, that the world, determines who they are. This is never the case.

Like all other factors or conditions, 'personality' is not an element that determines me, and it certainly cannot become my true self. But how strongly do we consider, feel, and believe that 'personality=me'? We must become aware of this. Personality is merely one 'tool' that we are born with and use throughout our lives, just like hair color, skin color, voice tone, height, and weight.

Furthermore, personalities only have different types; there are no better or worse personalities. The only difference lies in how effectively we utilize our personality. If you feel unfamiliar with your personality or unable to utilize it effectively, you can seek and implement methods to improve your relationship with it. The world offers numerous approaches to this challenge. The goal is to master these methods until they become as natural as using your limbs. This is both the foundation and the essence of the process. As long as this transformation doesn't occur and you persist in the belief that 'my personality is me,' meaningful change will remain elusive.

Second insight: identify, accept, and utilize your personality type. Rather than viewing it as a weakness to be compensated for, let's embrace our personality as a strength.

To effectively use and leverage personality as a tool, one must first gain a clear understanding of one's own personality. Many people believe they know their own personality well, but in reality, this is often not the case. Understanding one's personality means perceiving and comprehending oneself objectively, as others might see us.

If you are struggling with personality issues that persist despite your efforts, you must honestly acknowledge them. 'Ah, I don't truly understand my own personality!' That's precisely it. If you understood yourself well, you wouldn't feel so unresolved. 'Knowing that you don't know what you don't know' is the essential key.

There are various methods for identifying your personality traits. Using commercially available personality analysis systems to determine your type is a practical approach. Alternatively, you can utilize personality assessment systems offered at psychological counseling centers, psychiatric clinics, or coaching practices. We should neither place excessive trust in such personality systems nor dismiss them entirely. Simply acknowledge, 'Ah, this exists. I can interpret my personality roughly in this way,' and that is sufficient. Since these are merely 'tools,' do not passively accept them as presented. Instead, assume ownership and actively select, interpret, apply, and utilize the information.

The personality type systems that are widely recognized and utilized include MBTI, DISC, and Enneagram. Of course, there are many other tools available, but let's begin with these three for now. When searching the internet, you'll find numerous websites that offer real-time assessments. If utilizing free assessments, choose those with a greater number of survey questions. This will yield more accurate results.

Let's consider the MBTI system as an example. The system categorizes personality according to energy direction as 'Introverted (I)-Extroverted (E)'; primary perception method as 'Intuition (N)-Sensing (S)'; judgment criteria as 'Feeling (F)-Thinking (T)'; and implementation style as 'Perceiving (P)-Judging (J)'. These combinations create a classification of sixteen distinct personality types. For example, if your disposition selected from the four criteria is 'Introversion-Intuition-Feeling-Perception,' then you would be classified as an 'INFP' type. What's important here is not the personality type abbreviated in English letters, but understanding that you are introverted, your primary mode of perception is intuitive, your judgment method is feeling-based, and your lifestyle approach is perceptive.

It is quite valuable to also understand the characteristics of personality types opposite to your own across these four domains. Typically, we are familiar with our own personality and disposition, but often remain unaware of the feelings, dispositions, reactions, and thought processes that motivate others. Once you understand such personality type systems, you can discern why others behave the way they do.

A single assessment may not fully reveal your disposition or personality. In such cases, you can take multiple tests or try different assessment tools. With practice, you will gain better insight into how various systems classify personality traits. Furthermore, individuals rarely embody just one personality type. That is, I possess both 'introversion' and 'extroversion' elements, and similarly contain aspects of both 'intuition' and 'sensing'. Although I may have preferences or primarily utilize certain aspects, it's important to understand that a person's personality comprises multiple elements working in concert.

Since every personality type is unique and possesses its own strengths, we should—at least regarding personality—refrain from viewing traits as weaknesses to be corrected. Instead, consider that each trait can be a strength in itself, and focus on cultivating these inherent qualities. This perspective should be adopted from the outset.

For example,

It's not about being 'hypersensitive or overly reactive' but rather being 'perceptive and detail-oriented.'

It is not 'roughness' but 'boldness'.

It is not 'flusteredness' but 'agility'.

It is not 'timidity' but 'caution'.

It is not 'showing off' but 'having healthy high self-esteem'.

It is not 'nitpicking' but 'being analytical'.

It is not 'weakness' but 'friendliness and warmth'.

It is not 'frivolity' but 'liveliness and expressiveness'.

It is not 'shyness' but 'contemplation'.

It is not about being 'fastidious' but rather about being 'precise'.

It is not about being 'cold' but rather about being 'composed'.

It is not about being 'heartless' but rather about being 'objective'.

The reason we should focus on strengthening our strengths rather than compensating for weaknesses is because there are no inherent weaknesses in one's authentic personality. There is only the question of whether the individual utilizes their traits effectively or not. Any personality trait and its elements can become strengths when properly harnessed. Therefore, there is no need to fixate on traits you cannot use effectively by labeling them as weaknesses. That is merely a waste of time. You simply need to convert that trait back into its inherent strength. 'Transcending myself,' which will be discussed later, is also one method for achieving this. And as mentioned above, you should employ the strategy of intentionally reframing your personality characteristics—thinking of them not in terms of 'weaknesses' but deliberately in terms of 'strengths.' This is because your personality traits are fundamentally your strengths.

- You become the master of your personality when you transcend yourself

As emphasized multiple times earlier, your personality is not your 'self.' In many cases, people identify their personality with themselves, treating it as if it were inevitable. The same applies to how they view others. But I must emphasize: temperament or personality is merely a 'tool' that one uses.

Whether you live by using your personality as a tool or become buried within it is determined by whether or not you transcend yourself.

Though this sounds grandiose, it is neither complicated nor extraordinary nor special. It simply means not limiting or confining yourself to any restrictions that have previously been imposed upon you. There will be times when either I myself or others define or make assertions about me. The key is to use these characterizations as merely one piece of 'information' necessary for living, rather than regarding or accepting them as 'my entirety' or 'absolute truth'.

The realization is that my existence cannot be bound by any limitation or restriction, and that without such constraints, I always exist confidently and serenely just as I am now.

When we transcend ourselves in this way, how can our inherent temperament be transformed? For the sake of clarity, let's examine the four temperaments of the DISC personality system.

Each letter in DISC represents one of four personality types: 'Dominance, Influence, Steadiness, and Conscientiousness'. Let's observe how the same personality type transforms before and after self-transcendence.

For the Dominant type (D), before self-transcendence, individuals view their dominant personality as their entire identity and believe they cannot deviate from it, thus attempting to 'dominate every situation' regardless of whether they are right or wrong. Following someone else is not tolerated, and one cannot adapt to such situations. When others take the lead, there's an unsettling feeling that something will go wrong or mistakes will be made.

After transcending myself, I realize that my dominant temperament is not my entire being. I take the lead when necessary but refrain from doing so when it isn't needed. Initially I feel the desire to take control, but I can recognize this as merely my 'temperamental reaction' and stop myself. Even when I feel uncomfortable or anxious about not being in control, I recognize this as merely my automatic temperamental response, preventing further reactive behaviors. As time passes, one becomes better at distinguishing when to appropriately use a 'proactive temperament' and when not to, applying this knowledge more effectively.

The social type (I) can also be called the 'expressive type.' I feel truly alive and satisfied only when I express everything I feel, want to say, and want to do. I feel that acting this way is right.

After transcending myself, I notice that expression and an active disposition are merely one mode of existence. Of course, I believe expression is the voice of life, and expressing oneself is preferable to remaining silent. However, this principle requires discernment between appropriate and inappropriate moments for expression. This discernment allows us to distinguish between constructive and unconstructive forms of expression. Beyond the act of expression itself, one comes to understand its utility, effectiveness, and deeper meaning. Additionally, psychological maturity involves not only expressing oneself but also receiving and processing the expressions of others. One also recognizes that one's intrinsic value and meaning exist independently from one's expressions. Rather than becoming immersed in expressions, one knows how to utilize them as tools.

The Stable type (S) is generally friendly, peaceful, and tends to seek conformity. This disposition poses no problems in everyday situations; however, when one needs to take initiative or assert oneself, progress stalls or relationship difficulties emerge. They cannot comprehend why others criticize them when they believe they've been cautious and done nothing wrong.

After transcending myself, I recognize that the Stable type is 'merely my inherent temperament.' Therefore, even when it causes some discomfort, I take the initiative or express myself when situations require it. Of course, one's mind won't feel at ease, but this discomfort is merely a sensation without deeper significance— a truth we come to understand. The essence lies in how effectively we navigate situations and create meaningful relationships, not in our temperamental preference for harmonious circumstances. We also recognize that such harmonious relationships or situations are not inherently good or desirable in all instances.

The Cautious type (C) can also be referred to as the 'Analytical type'. They are meticulous in all matters and require everything to be logical and rational. Even when planning weekend recreational activities, they must have perfectly arranged supplies and schedules. They cannot tolerate anything abstract or ambiguous. For them, answers are always clearly defined, and they believe they possess this knowledge. Anything that lacks structure, precision, and meticulous organization or preparation is dismissed as incorrect or inauthentic. The problem lies in adhering to this even when it's unnecessary.

After transcending myself, I understand that 'perfection' is merely a constructed unity. I recognize that it is not something inherently existing but rather something created through 'necessity' and 'utility'. I understand that one's temperament is simply a useful tool when circumstances require it. When necessary, I employ my temperament to analyze meticulously, construct, and build up; but when unnecessary, I also know how to disregard rigid stages or sequences. Although it is not comfortable to do so, I recognize that this is merely an automatic response of my mind and has no correlation with reality.

Our goal is to thoroughly understand our temperament and personality, identify their strengths and weaknesses, and ultimately maximize our positive attributes.

Furthermore, our ultimate goal is not merely to remain confined within our temperament and personality, but to transcend them and become the master of ourselves. And to become the master of both myself and my temperament by 'transcending the self'. Transcending oneself is the most certain method of conquering and surpassing one's personality and temperament.

One need not perform grand actions to achieve such transformation. Rather, the opposite is true. We can utilize our personality as a resource and transform it so that it manifests as a strength. This is precisely what it means to transcend oneself. Therefore, instead of waiting to be changed, let us change ourselves. Rather than striving to change, let us simply choose change.

◆ ◆ ◆

Summary

Personality is not our true self but merely a tool we use in life. There is no good or bad in personality; what matters is how well you utilize it. One must understand and accept their personality, viewing it as a strength rather than a weakness. It is helpful to use personality type analysis tools to understand oneself objectively. The ultimate goal is to transcend personality and become its master. This can be achieved through the process of transforming personality traits into strengths.

3.7 The essence of life lies not in its content but in its utilization

: Wittgenstein's Wisdom

In September 2015, I encountered a touching story on the internet. It chronicled the remarkable experience of a Swedish four-person team that participated in the 'Adventure Racing World Championship' held in Ecuador in November 2014, and their meaningful encounter with a stray dog.

This championship is held annually and challenges participants to complete a grueling 700-kilometer journey over ten days, engaging in extreme sports including trekking, mountain biking, and kayaking, to determine who can finish the fastest.

The Swedish team devoted all their efforts to training for this competition. During the competition, the team discovered an emaciated dog on the road and, unable to ignore it, offered the dog some meatballs. The dog began following the team. Even through treacherous mountain trails and muddy terrain, the team worried about the dog's safety and attempted to leave it behind, but the dog refused to depart. At the final leg of the journey, where they needed to cross a 57 km river by kayak, the team bid farewell to the dog. The dog, seeing the boat departing, leaped into the river. Tim decided to take the dog aboard his kayak. Afterward, they continued the race at a reduced pace with the dog, eventually finishing in 12th place. Despite a year of rigorous training and the importance of competition results, they expressed no regret in gaining a precious friend instead of a trophy. The dog returned to Sweden with the team and became part of one team member's family. They named the dog 'Arthur.'

It is said that the philosopher Wittgenstein made this statement. "The essence of language lies not in its meaning (content) but in its application."

Now we can extend his words to declare the following.

"The essence of life lies not in its content but in how we utilize it."

A world championship that took a year to prepare for. If one prioritizes 'content,' then one must do their utmost and achieve the best possible results proportionate to their preparation. This is generally considered common sense. However, for the Swedish team, fixed 'content'—such as victory or favorable results—was not the essence of their participation in the competition. This applies not only to them but to all competition participants as well. In other words, the essence of competition lies not in winning or achieving good results, but rather in what one experiences through it and how these experiences can be utilized.

Our lives, and furthermore our existentiality, follow this same principle.

We believe that our lives—or our very selves—must be filled with predetermined content to be meaningful or complete. The numerous 'contents' determined personally, collectively, and socio-culturally eventually become beliefs as powerful as religion that imprison us. We are, in fact, our own jailers. It is the creator who becomes trapped in what they themselves have created. Who determines the content of such a life, my content? Is there an absolutely predetermined answer?

No!

Who dares to determine it?

Others and their ilk? The world and its judgments?

No one can determine it.

For convenience, we may define it, but we only use these

definitions and are never limited by them.

Not even by 'myself.'

What I achieve or fail to achieve, what kind of person I become or fail to become—these are merely 'content.' And the essence of life does not reside in its content. Content is merely one means of utilizing life. It is neither unique nor absolute. We will try to do all we can and achieve what we can, but all that content is merely a means, not an end.

As we live and exist, content naturally forms and accumulates. However, there is no predetermined content in life and existence that is 'the only meaningful thing.' It is created, but after experiencing it, we simply let it flow away. That choice is made by me, not by anyone else. That is our life. That is our existentiality.

While being able to create any content,
At the same time, not becoming captivated by that content.

Actively choosing the content.
Knowing that content is merely content.

I remain unattached to that content.
And utilizing life fully.

And
Since even the 'self' is content,
If possible,
Focus on utilizing even the 'self' effectively.

Summary

The essence of life lies not in content but in utilization. We often think that life must be filled with specific content to be meaningful, but this only limits us. The content of life is neither absolute nor fixed; it is what we choose and utilize. What's important is to create content without becoming bound by it, recognizing that content is merely content. Ultimately, we should be able to view life and even the 'self' as objects to be utilized.

3.8 The story of The Girl who suddenly discovered 'herself' one day

: Beyond All Names - Accepting True Identity

There was a girl.
And there was Mother.

Unfortunately, Mother, who was suffering emotionally,
called The Girl these names from a young age.

"Worthless girl,
Lazy girl,
Pretentious girl,
Selfish girl,
Ignorant girl,
Cunning girl.

Mother's voice, which The Girl had heard since childhood,
was absolute to The Girl,
so she couldn't conceive of any alternative.
And gradually, all these labels became her own self-perception.

The Girl's life was, unsurprisingly, difficult.
Especially when forming relationships with others.
The self-images she believed in
caused her tremendous suffering.
But she thought this suffering was normal.
Because that was how she perceived herself.

Then one day

The Girl was struck by a question.
'Are all these labels I identify with
truly who I am?'

Gradually,
she realized that her Mother's voice from childhood was not the
absolute truth
and when this realization crossed a threshold point,
the questioning began.

Not a 'question of negation' that simply rejects something, but
The question that transcends all negativity
was 'the inquiry of profound affirmation.'

And finally, she realized.

'The labels Mother attached
were never my true name!
That wasn't who I am.
It wasn't my authentic self.
Those things cannot limit or confine me.
I am not an existence defined or determined by such labels!'

In that moment,
she became free.

No, there was no need to become free.
Because there was nothing left to be confined by,
no need to escape or emerge from anywhere
Because I finally understood.

Just that all those past names, self-images,
things I believed constituted my identity
'were merely labels that a hurting Mother
attached to me within her unavoidable limitations'
As I realized this, all those names simply drifted away.

It wasn't that they needed to disappear or be erased,
but rather they became 'inconsequential.'
Because I now recognize their true nature.
Because I understand they are nothing of substance.

And The Girl discovered her authentic self.
From all the negative names of the past,
she became free.

Then something even more remarkable happened.
The Girl no longer needed names as she did in the past.
Because she realized that she
no longer needed to exist as 'merely a name'
she had noticed this truth.

Not just the negative names from the past,
but even the most positive names,
when attached to me who exists infinitely and freely,
the moment I confine myself to them,
the infinite me is forced into an extremely narrow name.
Because they realized that they would shrink.

The Girl now
Without needing any labels
So natural, confident, flexible,

Abundant, satisfied, lovable,
Relished her proud self-existence.
Simply enjoyed, savored, delighted in, allowed, and accepted.

Not rejecting all names
Whether negative or positive
Freely used names that were useful and necessary.

Sometimes just being 'myself',
Sometimes being a Mother,
Sometimes being a wife.
Sometimes becoming someone who helps others,
Sometimes becoming someone who receives help.

And throughout it all,
Regardless of these labels,
Always existed in my fundamental existence.

Already, inherently, always, effortlessly
Naturally, confidently,
Flexibly, abundantly,
Contentedly, lovingly,
With ease.

◆ ◆ ◆

Summary

The Girl lived trapped within the negative labels given by her Mother, until one day she realized these names were not her true identity. She discovers her essence by transcending all names and labels, learning to exist freely and naturally without being bound by any designation. While performing various roles according to necessity, she maintains her essential self, confidently accepting and enjoying her existence.

Chapter 4: Trauma - Not About Avoiding It But Making It Insignificant

4.1　Trauma is not something to eliminate, but to embrace and transcend

4.2　How to remain unhurt by others' words

4.3　How to become indifferent to 'that memory' that troubles you

4.4　When bad memories surface, it's actually an opportunity for growth

4.5　How to Liberate Yourself from Negative Emotions

4.6　Methods for Overcoming the Instinctive Fear of the Unfamiliar

4.7　To What Extent Am I 'Willingly' Experiencing Myself?

4.1 Trauma is not something to eliminate, but to embrace and transcend

Embracing and Transcending - The True Meaning of Healing

No one exists who has not experienced trauma in their heart. Relationships between people are like passing through a thornbush with bare skin; when relationships exist, trauma inevitably occurs in some form. And the timeline of that trauma continues to flow into the present.

We primarily receive trauma, but sometimes unintentionally inflict it as well. Even without specific intention or volition, trauma can emerge accidentally, situationally, or structurally. One person may cause trauma through carelessness or indifference, while another may experience trauma due to sensitivity or vulnerability. Of course, there are also instances where both parties bear responsibility.

While there are relatively minor wounds we exchange in daily life, there are also injuries that remain as profound psychological trauma. The 'physical, emotional, intellectual, and situational' shock, attacks, and violence that victims experience can be tremendously damaging. If you have had such experiences, psychological healing is absolutely necessary at some point, yet many people carry these burdens throughout their lives without seeking proper healing. According to neuroscience research, severe physical and mental violence, abuse, or shock experienced during childhood affects brain development and can lead to lifelong symptoms such as depression and anxiety. Therefore, it is advisable to seek professional help if possible.

There are cases where something that seems trivial to others can have an impact as serious as trauma on the person experiencing it.

In fact, this occurs surprisingly often. This is because emotional trauma is an internal matter for the person who experiences it. No matter how insignificant it may appear to others, if an individual perceives an experience as profound and serious, it genuinely becomes a major problem. When others fail to understand this aspect, the affected individual suffers additional distress.

Of course, unnecessary trauma that neither individuals nor society should experience must be eliminated to the greatest extent possible. This happens through individual maturation and structural societal improvements. This represents a task of both individual and social progress that must be achieved through collective cooperation. However, separate from these social efforts, the psychological trauma experienced by individuals is something we must process ourselves.

Ironically, individuals often make their own trauma more difficult to bear. This occurs because of a mindset that refuses to acknowledge already experienced trauma. Whether it occurred 10 years ago, 10 months ago, 1 hour ago, 10 seconds ago, or in this very moment, that trauma has already been experienced. My mind refuses to acknowledge the traumas and circumstances I've experienced.

"Why me? Why did this happen to me of all people? I did nothing wrong. It's unfair. I hate it." It's the voice within my inner self continuously shouting, "I cannot accept these experiences and traumas!"

This reaction is not incomprehensible. Just because you experienced something in the past doesn't mean you must unconditionally accept and permit it. Sometimes, by refusing to accept certain experiences, the mind becomes more at ease or finds satisfaction. It's a strategic mindset serving as a form of unity.

- One cannot deny what exists

The issue is duration. Or rather, the mental state that follows. What happens to our minds when we deny and refuse to acknowledge past situations, experiences, feelings, and the very existence of others?

Ultimately, it only makes things more difficult. This is because we inherently understand that attempting to believe something that exists does not exist is fundamentally a 'flawed approach.' Despite this awareness, we simply cannot cease our denial and rejection. Because if I permit and accept it, I will feel more miserable, wronged, and angry. However, since the experience and feelings of trauma remain intact in the brain's memory system, they may be 'repressed' but not 'erased.' Therefore, they continue to exert influence unconsciously. It is a process where the greater the conscious repression and neglect, the greater their influence becomes. Repression and neglect do not fundamentally solve the problem.

How should we address this dilemma? If you accept it, you feel wronged; if you don't accept it, you suffer. As long as humans remain social beings, psychological trauma arising from relationships cannot be avoided. Are we then inevitably destined to continue being wounded and suffering throughout our lives?

No. That cannot be so. Nor does it need to be. Even if experiencing trauma is unavoidable, there are actions we can take regarding the period of suffering that follows. Whether seeking professional counseling, overcoming challenges independently, or receiving support from those around us—all these approaches ultimately aim toward the same unity. 'It's not about avoiding trauma but recognizing its insignificance.' The trauma doesn't disappear, but eventually it becomes inconsequential. Well-being doesn't depend on the absence of trauma, but rather on reaching a state where its presence or absence no longer matters. Becoming unburdened by it. In other words, this is 'embracing and transcending.'

You might argue this sounds too simplistic, but that statement is by no means casual or thoughtless. Rather, it emerges from the most deliberate processes of healing, overcoming, empathy, and transcendence. It is a statement born of intense struggle. That's why it carries such power and gravity. It is also an affirmation of support—both for others and for ourselves.

Perhaps all the methods we attempt for healing psychological trauma—counseling, religion, prayer, social connections, programs, books, meditation, insight, time, and so forth—might merely be vehicles for achieving this ultimate purpose. While we certainly improve through such healing and insights, the essential transformation occurs when we realize that our trauma is not as overwhelming or significant as we had previously believed it to be.

In other words, this process involves relinquishing the absolute power we had unconsciously attributed to our past wounds. It means becoming free from the illusion that we believed was everything. It means reducing the importance we once assigned to it. And it means growing larger than that trauma, larger than the memories of the past.

If there are wounds in your heart, let us commit fully to healing them. Seeking counseling does not signify dependence on others nor an inability to be self-reliant. Just as we willingly seek treatment for physical wounds at a hospital, we should confidently seek assistance for our psychological trauma. Beyond this, let us explore the various other methods that are available to us. Therefore, let us heal our psychological trauma through our own methods. This process is simultaneously a process of growth and expansion. That is how it should be approached.

Let us examine this aspect clearly. Healing does not occur merely by addressing the cause of the trauma. Becoming free from these causes by properly addressing them is one path to unity, but now let us delve deeper. The fundamental principle of healing lies in this: I remained wounded because I attributed importance to the trauma and remained confined within existing frameworks. True healing occurs when I grow beyond these limitations, no longer remain trapped by them, achieve freedom, embrace the experience, and transcend it—ultimately transforming 'trauma into non-trauma.'

Let us strengthen and mature ourselves so that we may avoid re-experiencing past traumas in our present and future. And regarding past traumas, let us achieve freedom not by seeking ways to liberate ourselves, but by clearly recognizing their insignificance, thus naturally attaining liberation.

◆ ◆ ◆

Summary

Every person experiences psychological trauma. Denying or ignoring trauma does not resolve the issue but rather exacerbates it. True healing is not about erasing trauma, but acknowledging and overcoming it. This is the process of realizing that trauma no longer defines us, and growing beyond its limitations. Rather than merely addressing the causes of trauma, it is more important to transform our perception of and response to the traumatic experience. Finding and utilizing various healing methods, including seeking professional help, can be profoundly beneficial in this journey.

4.2 How to remain unhurt by others' words

: Permitting both my freedom and yours simultaneously

Some individuals are particularly vulnerable to trauma from others' words. Ideally, I would prefer to confront the situation immediately, expressing myself candidly and moving forward. However, depending on one's personality, even this approach can be challenging. Consequently, I later find myself ruminating in solitude, feeling wronged and resentful.

Is there a viable solution?

Multiple approaches exist, and regardless of which method one chooses, the essential elements are consistent practice and persistent effort. In this text, we will examine one particularly powerful method among these approaches.

Before proceeding, there is a fundamental premise: never allow yourself to become a fool. If you are being unjustly attacked or find yourself in an unfair situation, you should naturally respond and express yourself in some appropriate manner. If necessary, you may respond in kind, verbally defend yourself, or even respond physically. Do whatever needs to be done, whatever you wish to do, or whatever you are capable of doing. Do not remain passive.

Beyond (or simultaneously with) your justified reaction, implement this approach. If you are easily traumatized by others' words or actions and tend to hold onto them for a long time, from now on, make this declaration within your heart.

"All your thoughts, words, and actions are naturally your freedom.

Therefore, I grant you your freedom!

Grant this freedom with complete dignity, as the master of your relationships and circumstances. It is their freedom, after all—what right do I have to interfere? Just as no one has the right to dictate my actions, I extend the same respect to others. This doesn't mean remaining passive regardless of how the other person behaves. First, it means adopting a mindset that acknowledges his freedom. Always remember that you can freely choose your own actions, independently of his.

When someone treats us inconsiderately, we typically endure it outwardly while inwardly fuming, 'This really upsets me. You shouldn't behave this way.' Though we may not express it, in our hearts we refuse to accept anything from the other person. We are exercising a subtle form of dictatorship within our minds. It is not merely a simple metaphor; individuals with social power sometimes manifest the dictatorship within their minds as actual dictatorship in reality.

When viewed wisely, internal prohibitions and disallowances yield neither effect nor benefit. Such attempts neither stop the other person nor create meaningful change. They only leave us feeling more aggrieved. This is because it is fundamentally impossible for us to prohibit another's freedom of thought, speech, and action. When we persist in attempting the impossible, we only burden our minds with suffering while resolving nothing. We must become aware of this pattern.

This is not the end. It cannot be. It's not just about considering the other person; for the sake of fairness in relationships, 'I' must naturally be considered too. Because to myself, I am also 'others' who deserve to be treated fairly. Allow others their freedom while also allowing your own. Therefore, declare in your heart:

"All my thoughts, words, and actions are naturally my freedom.
I permit my freedom!

I am first granting permission to my own freedom, even without the permission of others. While doing so, you simultaneously grant the other person freedom in your heart. It is about enjoying your own freedom while acknowledging the other person's right to theirs.

Now, let us permit freedom for both sides! Gradually, you will notice your mindset and behavioral patterns becoming distinctly different from before. You become more open, magnanimous, liberated, and in harmony with yourself and others. Both parties can express themselves freely and accept one another unconditionally.

Initially, these two actions may appear to be in conflict. Isn't it contradictory that I allow myself to respond freely while also permitting the other person their freedom? This might create some psychological confusion. 'How should I handle situations when I need to prohibit someone else's behavior? Should I prohibit it or not?' Questions like these arise.

Let's examine a specific example of how to navigate such situations. In certain circumstances, I may feel compelled to exclaim 'No!' or 'Stop that!' in response to another person's words or actions. Now, independently of that person, allow yourself to genuinely grant them the freedom to express themselves in such a way within your heart. 'Yes, that is your freedom!' Then, also grant yourself the same freedom.

Does this sound like mere wordplay? However, in reality, there is a clear distinction from how things were before. Previously, I wanted to say 'no' or 'don't do that,' but unable to grant myself this freedom, I forcibly endured while suppressing my feelings of resentment. Whether I spoke up or remained silent, I did not truly allow the other person the freedom to express themselves. This crucial difference will become clear to you. Now it's about granting freedom to others while also freely saying 'No!' or 'Don't do that!'

myself. Of course, I can also choose not to say such things.

Though they may appear similar on the surface, these two approaches are completely different. The latter is much more liberating, refreshing, and open. Moreover, it is far more effective and leads to different outcomes in how situations unfold. In the past, my heart was closed and I lacked psychological flexibility, causing me to respond in ways that consistently worsened situations and relationships. Now, I'm beginning to see myself, others, and my surroundings from a broader perspective. This allows us to think and act with greater flexibility, making new solutions more apparent. We may even develop the ability to skillfully navigate challenging situations with gentle humor.

What is our typical response? We deny others their freedom of expression. Whether we explicitly say 'don't do that' or not, our internal state remains the same. Consequently, my discomfort persists, and the tension or negative emotions between us fail to dissipate.

Or conversely, while allowing freedom for others' actions, we tell ourselves, 'No. I must restrain myself.' 'It's not acceptable to feel anger, nor to express it,' we might tell ourselves. When my mind is in this state, whether I verbalize 'don't do that' to the other person or not makes no difference. The tension and negative emotions remain unresolved.

Allowing freedom for both sides is, metaphorically speaking, like transforming the playground. If my existing mindset was like a tilted, bumpy, and dirty playground where proper play was impossible, it now becomes flat, even, and clean—a space where authentic interaction can occur. Upon this foundation, one can move more freely and joyfully through life.

Initially, permitting freedom on both sides may feel unfamiliar and awkward; arguments might intensify, and you may experience moments of doubt thinking, 'This doesn't seem right.' It might appear that little has changed from the past. However, as you grow more accustomed to this approach, transformation occurs. If you persevere without surrendering, your expertise will develop and you will become more proficient.

One key strategy is to engage with what you can accomplish now rather than waiting for significant change, while maximizing your enjoyment of the process. Everything is successful 'to the extent' that I pursue it. If I achieve a level of 1, then it is a success at level 1. The same principle applies to level 10. It is not necessarily true that only achieving a success level of 100 constitutes meaningful success.

What's more fascinating is that new qualitative changes can continue to emerge progressively. Each stage offers its own unique form of fulfillment. 'Ah, so this is what it means to permit freedom on both sides simultaneously!' This realization doesn't occur just once but can expand and renew itself multiple times. Perhaps if you experience an 'Ah!' moment in your consciousness while reading this text, it may indicate that the first qualitative change has already begun in our Unconscious, our subconscious mind. The key is to avoid becoming prematurely discouraged or giving up simply because you don't succeed at first.

There are two distinct stages to learning how to ride a bicycle. The theoretical learning stage and the practical riding stage. This concludes the theoretical explanation of 'allowing both my freedom and your freedom in order to avoid trauma from others' words.' Now, let's venture out and actually ride the bicycle. Let's continue riding even if we fall occasionally. Isn't that precisely how one learns to ride a bicycle? If you persist, you will soon see yourself running with enthusiasm. Who knows? You might even find yourself running joyfully from the very beginning. Furthermore, this represents 'great courage' for the pursuit of happiness in one's life. Moreover, it is the courage to find happiness not only for oneself but also with one's beloved partner, family, friends, and acquaintances. Therefore, let us proceed while offering ourselves encouragement.

◆ ◆ ◆

Summary

A powerful approach for those who are easily traumatized by others' words is to 'simultaneously honor both others' freedom and your own freedom.' One must acknowledge others' thoughts, words, and actions as their freedom while simultaneously allowing oneself the same freedom. This enables one to develop a broader perspective on situations and facilitates more liberated and constructive responses. Practicing this method may feel awkward initially, but with time, one can experience qualitative changes in managing relationships and navigating situations. This represents a courageous approach toward securing happiness for both oneself and others.

4.3 How to become indifferent to 'that memory' that troubles you

: Applying this method not only to negative emotions and thoughts but to all emotions and thoughts

The experience of unwanted feelings or thoughts repeatedly surfacing can be extremely challenging. The words and actions of someone who behaved disagreeably a few days ago continue to resurface in my mind. Each time, the feelings of humiliation and anger are fully experienced again. 'Ah, I should have expressed my anger or refuted them in this way...' or 'How dare they disrespect me over something so trivial...', 'I should have done this instead...' Just when it seems forgotten, it resurfaces again, and again when it seems forgotten, it returns once more. Some memories cling persistently, refusing to fade even after months or years have passed.

While current problems and worries about the future frequently visit us, it is particularly the 'remnants of our past' that strongly and repeatedly resurface. Negative experiences from the past, along with the emotions and thoughts we experienced then, continue to influence our present. Even in the midst of joy, these memories can suddenly emerge, ruining our mood, stripping away our confidence, and dampening the atmosphere. Even though they are things that have already passed, things that are dead.

These feelings and thoughts seem to be beyond our control. It's not that I consciously feel or recall them, but rather they appear to spring up within me of their own accord. Is there no way to free ourselves from these intrusions? Must we perpetually suffer from unwanted feelings and thoughts that arise at any moment?

Certainly not. There is a method.

To transform any habit, two processes are essential. One is 'awareness (insight)' and the other is 'specific methodology'. It involves recognizing the existing flaws and using specific methods to transform them.

- Just because something is felt or comes to mind does not mean it is 'important'

Our consciousness subtly leads us to believe that things we feel or that arise in our minds are 'important'. This is predominantly an unconscious reaction. In other words, this is not the result of intentional consciousness, but rather something that has been conditioned since childhood. We must clearly recognize this pattern.

Just as dream content is random, the thoughts that arise in our consciousness during the day are also largely random. This interpretation is supported by neuroscience as well. Of course, if we delve deeper, we might uncover the fundamental reasons why certain feelings or thoughts arise, but most of the time we cannot know for certain. It's similar to how we cannot precisely determine why yesterday's dream was composed of those specific contents. We may make various interpretations, but strictly speaking, they are all merely inferences.

Particularly feelings, moods, emotions, or thoughts arising from past negative experiences are even more perplexing. Why, while quietly studying, walking down the street, working, or driving, does that particular person suddenly come to mind, triggering unpleasant feelings? Things that serve no purpose to remember.

As I have already stated, it is arbitrary. It is random. There is no reason. It simply happens.

The problem lies in how we unconsciously or automatically attach a post-interpretation of 'this is important' to such random occurrences. We must understand this point. We need to develop insight into this phenomenon. And from this moment forward, we must actively reframe our thoughts to: 'Although I feel this and it comes to mind right now, it is not important!'

Attributing importance to these thoughts is self-deception. I am allowing myself to be misled by my own mind. It is a misconception to assume there must be some underlying reason or necessity for these thoughts. Let us no longer be deceived or misled by them. If something were truly important, it would not only be strongly felt and arise in our consciousness, but it would also help us, improve our situation, or resolve an issue. However, this is clearly not the case. Rather, it becomes more confusing and only makes me feel worse.

Let's declare once again, strongly and clearly.

"Just because I feel something or it comes to mind does not mean it is 'important'!"

Of course, at first, even when you say this, deep in your heart the thought will persist: 'There must be a reason why I feel and think about this. It must be important' - these existing conscious and unconscious impressions will continue to arise. Because it is a conscious habit that has been maintained for ten or several decades, it cannot be changed overnight.

The more properly and consciously you notice it, the faster it changes and disappears. Let's not simply say, 'I guess that's just how it is.' Then you have no power, and nothing changes. 'Not important?' You need to develop self-awareness through your own power while also questioning, 'Why is that?' 'Is what I feel and recall truly important?' Am I unconsciously believing this? 'Is that really so?' You must doubt and break through these barriers with your own strength. If this doesn't work, the subsequent process cannot proceed.

- Becoming increasingly indifferent (unconcerned) about what is felt and what arises

Now it has become somewhat clear to me that the negative feelings, moods, emotions, and thoughts that suddenly arise are 'not important.' So what comes next?

Even with clear self-awareness, these feelings do not disappear in an instant. This is because traces of them still remain in my mind or heart. The neural network of those feelings and thoughts still remains in the brain. Therefore, signals can continue to flow until the network weakens to a certain degree. When these signals flow and activate, I experience and recall these feelings again. This is why specific methods are necessary.

Methods to properly process what we feel and what emerges in our consciousness.

The key is to become emotionally detached from what we feel and what surfaces in our minds.

To become apathetic toward them.

To develop a sense of disinterest.

When I believed that the emotions I unconsciously experienced and the thoughts that spontaneously arose were 'important,' I naturally had no choice but to place significant weight on them. So I repeatedly experienced the negative feelings that accompanied memories of that person who mistreated me, their actions, and those painful situations. Foolishly.

Now I consciously understand that these thoughts are not important and have no real meaning (this self-awareness needs to be continuously reinforced until it becomes sufficiently clear. It doesn't happen automatically or without effort). Then naturally, I will give less of my mind's attention, meaning, concern, and mental energy that I had previously invested in those individuals.

Initially, as some inertia from the past remains, I might unknowingly become excited and immersed again, falling back into previous patterns. But there is a world of difference between acting with awareness versus acting unconsciously. Now I possess that awareness. I no longer automatically attribute importance to something merely because I feel it or it surfaces in my consciousness. Rather, I recognize that it is insignificant, unremarkable, and holds no particular value.

The better you become at this, the more indifferent you grow toward those negative thoughts. You become dispassionate. You become unconcerned. If this doesn't come naturally, practice it intentionally. You must. Through repeated practice of this response, you'll eventually reach a point where you no longer feel disturbed even when those thoughts arise or resurface.

- Whether you mind them or not becomes irrelevant

Beyond this approach, there exists an even more powerful method. Even if those thoughts are felt, recalled, or continue to demand your attention, develop indifference toward the very 'feeling, recalling, and attending' itself. Don't feel disappointed or burdened because you care, and don't worry about the need to stop caring. This could easily become yet another psychological trap.

In other words, when instructed not to care about something, you now find yourself caring about your inability to stop caring. So as you become caught again, trapped, and blocked, this itself becomes a burden. I shouldn't allow my mind to be captured by the emotions and thoughts that arise. Telling yourself, 'I shouldn't keep worrying or struggling because of these things.'

You don't need to try to let go of those feelings and thoughts. Letting go happens as a result, not because you set 'letting go' as your goal. Simply notice them instead. Acknowledge them, accept them, and embrace them. If that proves difficult, simply make the choice to do so. The result is the same. Instead of maintaining your conscious stubbornness, patterns, habits, and tendencies that insist 'my thoughts and feelings are important,' choose to believe 'just because I think and feel something doesn't necessarily mean it's important.'

There is a crucial point that should not be overlooked here. This approach applies not just to negative feelings and thoughts, but to 'all feelings and thoughts.' How can we consider most feelings and thoughts as important and meaningful, while treating only the negative ones as insignificant? This is simply not possible.

It's perfectly acceptable even if your awareness is initially faint and weak. At first, simply acknowledge it with an 'Ah, I see~'. That's sufficient. Then gradually work to make this awareness clearer. As you practice this, it will naturally become increasingly distinct.

There is an inevitable response that emerges whenever I write this type of content.

"So, what exactly should I do and how? Please provide me with specific guidance."

"I've diligently tried both approaches, but neither has been particularly helpful."

I understand completely. You're right. It's perfectly natural to have such questions or doubts.

The answer to that is as follows. As mentioned earlier, you must first develop a clear 'awareness' of your situation. In other words, it means 'breaking free from existing misconceptions and embracing more accurate perspectives.' It is about 're-perception' and changing one's thought patterns. This is possible because the problematic existing stereotypes were also formed within me through the same process. Since I've done it in the past, it's possible this time too. However, this time it's about restoring to the original state. Change is possible. We must be careful though—it's not merely about changing thoughts. It's about discarding what was previously incorrect so that what is inherently right can naturally emerge. Therefore, it's not about striving to change, but about reclaiming what was originally there.

Is it easy? Certainly not. Therefore, one must actively change and reframe one's own thoughts and feelings. This is something only you yourself can do. Why? Because you alone are the master of your own mind. No one can do it for you. Guidance and techniques can be shared, but ultimately it is you who must take direct action. This is an immutable truth.

After perception has changed, one must address past habits and inertia through concrete implementation. Repetition and effort are necessary, but if you have confidence that it works, it won't be as difficult as it might seem. Therefore, let's continue without stopping until the moment we cross the threshold point of actual change. This is true of all processes that pursue transformation.

◆ ◆ ◆

Summary

The method of becoming indifferent to traumatic memories includes two key processes: 'perception (insight)' and 'specific techniques'. First, you need to recognize that the thoughts or emotions that arise in your mind are not inherently significant. These are mostly random and meaningless things. Next, one must practice specific methods to become indifferent to these thoughts and emotions. This means not giving them attention or attributing importance to them. This process applies to all emotions and thoughts.

4.4. When bad memories surface, it's actually an opportunity for growth

: Breaking the Vicious Cycle - How to Stop Repeating Painful Memories

The brain tends to repeatedly revive unpleasant memories or mental trauma even when we are at rest. Naturally, we suffer whenever memories resurface. Are you aware of this fact? That moment is precisely a valuable opportunity for us to properly process that memory. In other words, we can engage in 'self-psychological healing'. What does it mean that the emergence of unpleasant memories presents an opportunity for healing?

- Why does our brain repeatedly bring up unpleasant memories?

First, let's consider why past events spontaneously come to mind. For instance, it could be a 'self-protection mechanism' that causes us to ruminate on previously experienced negative events to ensure greater caution in the future. Another reason is that our minds cannot accept what has already occurred, causing us to yearn for alternative scenarios, if only in our imagination. In this process, we unintentionally perpetuate the memory through repetition. The initial purpose is to alleviate frustration, but it ultimately transforms into lingering attachment and obsession. This is primarily caused by feelings of resentment, anger, sadness, or regret associated with the event.

First, let us examine the case of the 'self-protection mechanism.' While this mechanism is inherently beneficial, it becomes problematic when past memories resurface with excessive frequency. In other words, it's acceptable to have moderate recollections or to exercise caution to avoid similar experiences, but problems arise when these memories create emotional burden or confusion.

In such instances, one should avoid becoming immersed in the emotions associated with recalled memories, and instead objectively utilize them to remain vigilant in the future. This is the fundamental purpose and rationale of 'recollection,' which should be intentionally recognized, and it's advisable not to employ it for other purposes. Despite potential difficulties, this process must be undertaken deliberately and consciously. Otherwise, one will merely re-experience unpleasant feelings as before, reinforcing negative internal experiences. (The neural synapse network associated with that specific memory is actually strengthened.)

Second, 'wishing for different circumstances in the past—the resolution of unfulfilled desire'—is essentially 'wishing for the impossible.' While I fully understand this sentiment, it represents a highly inefficient strategy. Or rather, it is selfish in a misguided way. It is entirely possible to prepare for the present and future more wisely and confidently based on past experiences. Yet beyond this, wanting to change the past itself represents excessive desire. One must tell oneself to cease pursuing impossible wishes for one's own well-being. This represents a genuinely selfish response that serves one's true interests.

Now, we must examine another dimension of this issue. This presents an excellent opportunity for 'self-psychological healing.'
In Neuroscience, there exists a theory known as 'Neuroplasticity.' This theory posits that the synapse networking of brain cells transforms in response to appropriate stimulation. Let us first examine the following figure.

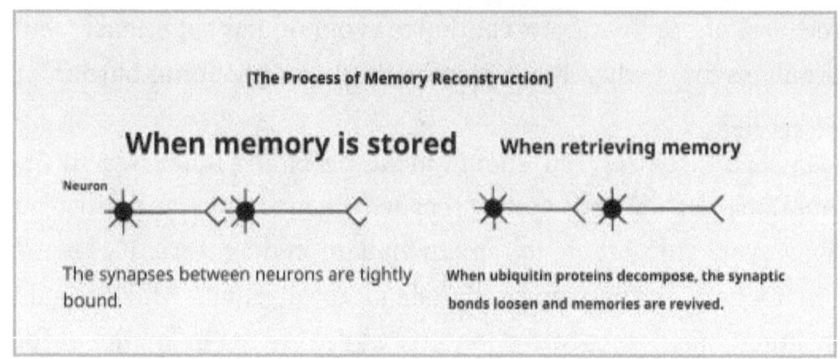

In this simple yet essential diagram, the critical point we must note is where 'synaptic bonds loosen when memories are retrieved.' And when synapses loosen, an opportunity for neuronal rearrangement emerges.

In other words, when unpleasant memories from the past surface and we re-experience the emotions or situations from that time, the neural network—the synaptic network—of that memory loosens, which means we have the opportunity to rearrange that neural network. Therefore, when memories resurface, when we re-experience them, and when we feel them strongly again, these moments become opportunities for self-psychological healing.

Wouldn't it be advantageous when recalled memories and emotions are more vivid and intense? The more intense this experience, the more actively synapses are loosened, thereby increasing opportunities for meaningful change. When we recall memories dispassionately or engage in simple reminiscence, the emotional response is weak, indicating minimal loosening of synaptic bonds. Consequently, opportunities for transformation are diminished.

When negative memories and traumas from the past unconsciously surface, most of us become immersed in those emotions, struggling through the same experience again, merely closing our neural networks rather than pursuing concrete healing and transformation. In this process, we only strengthen the synapses associated with negative emotions and reactions. This is a reaction that almost everyone unconsciously engages in. Rather than helping, it actually exacerbates the situation.

We have discovered the secret that when we deliberately recall past memories, the bonds of the corresponding synapses begin to loosen. When synaptic bonds loosen, an opportunity for change presents itself. Therefore, we should no longer unconsciously and automatically re-experience negative feelings, reinforce them, and close off memories as we did in the past. Rather, when these feelings arise, we should recognize, 'Ah, this is an opportunity for healing!' and respond appropriately to dissolve these bonds. Then, even though 'the facts of the past (memories)' remain unchanged, 'our responses (connections in the synaptic network)' will be transformed. When our reactions change in this way, even though the facts of the past (memories) remain, they no longer matter to us. Gradually, we become indifferent to them. We have already become free.

- Methods for Transforming Unconscious Memory Repetition into a Healing Process

Whether through self-protection mechanisms or mechanisms of unfulfilled desires, we have discovered that our brain's replay of memories can become an opportunity for healing and transformation. Rather than unconsciously re-experiencing and reinforcing patterns as in the past, it involves breaking existing synaptic networks or replacing them with new ones. How specifically should we approach this?

The most important thing to remember is the 'feeling'. This is because 'feeling equals the loosening of synapses'. That is, when we experience feeling A, the synaptic network corresponding to A loosens, and when we experience feeling B, the synaptic binding corresponding to B loosens. We must recognize this feeling by subdividing it into two categories. The first category consists of the five senses (五感), which are the most basic physical sensations we consider as feelings. The second category is emotional feeling. In other words, this is what we express as our moods and emotions. Now, when unpleasant memories, experiences, and trauma surface, let's try this approach.

First, intentionally re-perceive the situation to 'separate and neutralize past feelings.'

When that memory replays, if you simply repeat the experience and feel the same emotions without intervention, it actually becomes reinforced. We can control the unconscious with our conscious awareness. Although these memories may be so intense that they inevitably resurface despite our best efforts. At these moments, it is essential to intentionally perceive the situation as follows: 'A re-experiencing of memory is occurring now. But I will not blindly re-experience it as I did before.' By intentionally adopting this perspective, the automatic emotional responses to that event can gradually diminish.

Initially, past reactions may continue to repeat themselves without any noticeable change. That is, until reaching the threshold point of change—until 'the change in that synapse' occurs to a significant degree—the re-experiencing that happened in the past will continue to recur. The most effective response in such situations is to recognize that it is 'merely inertia.' When I recall that situation or that person, I still feel troubled, angry, resentful, embarrassed, and sad, but this is merely because those feelings remain. It is simply a reaction occurring as the synaptic bonds loosen, and recognizing this perception is key.

Second, it is about not minding even when you feel these emotions. It is about not assigning importance to them. From the beginning, we ourselves were the ones who assigned importance to these feelings.

As the intentional re-perception mentioned earlier becomes clearer, the emotional reactions that were automatically immersed in the past will gradually weaken. The key is not to become discouraged and abandon the process midway. Emotions will naturally continue to be felt until the synaptic connections are reorganized to a sufficient degree. This is entirely normal. Disappointment leads to cessation, but now that you understand this principle, you can continue the process without interruption by avoiding discouragement.

In such situations, one should respond by 'feeling without attaching importance.' This means not assigning significance to the emotion. We unconsciously believe that when thoughts or feelings arise, they must be important. Previously, I unknowingly assigned 'significance' to past events that occasionally surfaced in my mind, but now I consciously choose not to do this. This does not mean that the past event itself lacks importance. I am not suggesting you ignore it. Rather, I am advising you to cease 'the unconscious habit of attributing importance to the very act of remembering and feeling.'

Third, intentionally recall or experience neutral or opposing feelings and situations. While the first two methods alone can produce a significant self-healing effect, adding this third method solidifies the transformation. The previous two methods sometimes naturally progress to this process. Rather than allowing synapses associated with past 'anxiety, dissatisfaction, resentment, embarrassment, sadness, anger' to activate, the more consciously you recognize and reperceive them, the more naturally the old synaptic networks disconnect or weaken. Furthermore, this neutralization or balancing process can be strengthened even more. The common phrase 'It's okay to not be okay!' can be considered related to this process. This is not 'unfounded positivity,' but rather a very specific practice that actually transforms the synaptic networks in the brain.

The 'neutral feeling and state' also refers to a 'comfortable, quiet, and safe feeling and state.' Therefore, meditation techniques that facilitate such states can be particularly helpful. The more we create and experience such states, the weaker our previous anxious and negative memories (synaptic networks) become.

Let's take this a step further and more actively recall or experience the opposite feelings and situations. This is also known as 'visualization' or 'imagining'. This is a method of intentionally recalling positive and beneficial experiences, memories, sensations, and emotions, rather than automatically repeating the negative sensory experiences and emotions from the past when a troubling memory resurfaces.

This method is not easy to practice alone, so you may benefit from seeking professional assistance. A knowledgeable healer or counselor can provide specific suggestions and guidance to facilitate positive feelings and experiences. With your eyes closed, you follow their guidance while fully embodying these feelings and experiences.

When unpleasant memories and experiences inadvertently surface and begin to consume us, we must break the pattern of unconscious repetition. Rather, let us consider this as an opportunity to consciously re-examine our perceptions and implement change.

This is something worth attempting for my own benefit and for the improvement of my life.

Summary

When negative memories surface, they can be transformed into opportunities for healing. According to the theory of neuroplasticity, when memories are recalled, synaptic connections become malleable, making reconstruction possible. Utilizing this principle, we can respond in the following three ways:

1) Separate and neutralize past emotions,

2) Refrain from attributing excessive importance to emotions,

3) Deliberately recalling neutral or opposing emotions.

Through this process, one can diminish the impact of negative memories and facilitate psychological healing.

4.5 How to Liberate Yourself from Negative Emotions

: Emotions persist because we cling to them

Emotions present a significant challenge for everyone. Rather than the emotions themselves, what matters is how we handle and regulate them. As an aside, it is said that certain Western meditation traditions view humans as being composed of three distinct bodies. The first is the most familiar to us, the 'physical body.' It refers to our material form. The second is the 'emotional body.' This views the human emotional system as a unified body. The third is the 'mental body.' It is the entity responsible for cognitive functions.

Even setting aside mystical elements, it is fascinating to view human composition as three components: body, emotion, and thought. From a neurological perspective, could we correspond the deepest parts of our brain such as the brain stem and medulla to the physical body, the limbic system to the emotional body, and the cerebral cortex to the mental body? This text focuses on emotion among these three aspects. How can we better understand and manage the emotional elements that constitute our being?

The true nature of emotions, the role they have played and how they have evolved during the evolutionary process, and how they manifest are being scientifically revealed through research on neuroscience and hormonal influences. In this text, we will examine how to effectively process emotions that have already emerged, particularly negative emotions, and what methods can be employed to prevent experiencing similar emotional distress in the future. In essence, 'emotional regulation' is our central theme.

- Do not reject, stop, or try to change emotions that are already

being felt

The most challenging aspect of dealing with negative emotions that arise within me is that it is not easy to stop them or transform them into other emotions. No, it is almost impossible. The reason is simple: the emotion has, quite literally, 'already occurred'. Physiologically speaking, the neural networks that trigger that emotion have already fired, and hormones and other substances have already been secreted and dispersed throughout the body. We cannot change physical phenomena that have already occurred through mere mental effort. Therefore, the first principle to bear in mind regarding emotional issues is as follows:

'Do not reject, suppress, or attempt to change emotions you are already experiencing.'

Rather than trying to manage the emotions you feel, instead cease the very 'impulse to manage them'—abandon the desire to change what is already present. Attempting the impossible not only leads to inevitable failure but also generates additional secondary suffering. While already struggling with primary emotions, you inadvertently create secondary emotions. This compounds your distress in multiple ways.

Nevertheless, 'the desire to somehow manage our emotions' is not as easy to relinquish as it might sound. This stems from the deeply held beliefs and inherent stubbornness of our minds. It is due to our persistent belief that emotions can be controlled, and our stubborn insistence that they should be controlled.

There is a quote often attributed to Einstein that circulates widely. "Insanity is doing the same thing over and over again and expecting different results." Whether these are truly his words remains uncertain, but the sentiment is remarkably apt. How foolish it would be to expect success while repeatedly employing a methodology that has already failed in scientific experiments. Emotional regulation follows the same principle. If it's a 'working method,' one should persevere without giving up, but adhering to ineffective approaches only invites self-inflicted suffering.

Another reason we cannot abandon our attempts to change our emotions is the mindset that 'I will not acknowledge the existence of emotions I am already experiencing.' That I experience such emotions—I cannot permit myself to accept their existence.

One of the most challenging behaviors that complicates our lives is the act of denying the existentiality of something that already exists. Of course, it is valid to reject contradictions or inequalities in individuals or society that should rightfully be corrected or eliminated. Here, we are discussing personal psychological habits. This applies not only to emotions, but also to people, situations, and even to ourselves.

For instance, in our families, friendships, schools, workplaces, and other communities, we often must maintain relationships with individuals we dislike or with whom we are incompatible. The greatest mistake we commit in such moments is denying another person's existential worth. The sentiment that says, 'You don't belong in this family, friend circle, school, company, church, temple, or academic community!' The feeling that declares, 'I cannot acknowledge your right to exist!'

If I possess sufficient power or capability, I might push that person away. This occasionally happens. Yet whether or not I can do this, something more fundamental remains at stake. The reality is that both myself and the other person fulfill specific roles within that community, and each of us occupies a unique position within it. Therefore, neither I nor the other person can be easily dismissed or eliminated. This is because it is not merely an individual problem but also, to some extent, an issue of 'collective construction'. It is similar to how one cannot carelessly remove any part from a car. If you become immersed solely in personal perspectives and emotions and begin to deny others, your life within the community becomes difficult. Naturally, it becomes difficult for others as well. Eventually, interpersonal issues can escalate into organizational problems. All these are adverse effects that occur from 'denying the existentiality of what already exists'. It occurs because we desire what is impossible.

The best approach is to first acknowledge the existentiality of the person as they already exist. To initially accept and allow their being. Although the taste may be bitter and the heart reluctant, simply refraining from pursuing the impossible is already a significant gain. By avoiding unnecessary energy depletion, the mind gradually stabilizes and finds inner peace. Once this composure is established, the possibility of naturally discovering appropriate solutions for oneself, others, and the entire community greatly increases.

This is not about denying or avoiding the truth. Avoidance is never the answer in any situation. Rather, it is about calming your mind for your own well-being. Then you can view potential solutions with greater clarity and openness.

After doing this, make your choice freely. There are no limitations to the solution you choose. You need not always seek the most amicable outcome. You may cut ties with the other person, engage in discussion, or offer guidance. Alternatively, it can be transformed into a positive relationship, or if necessary, one can maintain indifference. If it is the optimal approach, it can be applied regardless of whether the relationship is negative or positive. First, this is only possible when there exists 'an acceptance of the other's existentiality' as the foundation of one's mindset. There is a profound difference between having this acceptance and lacking it.

The reason I have elaborated on this matter is because my emotions function in the same way. If you substitute 'the other' in the previous discussion with 'my emotions,' all situations remain identical. Therefore, what we must do to 'liberate ourselves from negative emotions' is this.

It is not about changing or stopping emotions, but about becoming comfortable with feeling any emotion. In other words, it means allowing any emotion to appear as it is. It means acknowledging it. It means accepting it. It means not being troubled by it. It means simply experiencing it without denial or affirmation, without being swayed or consumed by it.

The 'comfort' mentioned here is not the 'comfort' in the sense of 'comfortable or uncomfortable,' but a state that embraces and transcends both conditions. In other words, it is similar to the concept of 'non-attachment' discussed in Buddhist Zen traditions. Usually, the most problematic aspect when practicing this is 'becoming attached to non-attachment.' That is, while attempting to practice non-attachment to various situations encountered in daily life or during meditation, one repeatedly becomes attached. And one becomes uncomfortable and anxious about that 'attachment,' thus becoming attached again. What is the solution to this? Naturally, it is 'not becoming attached to non-attachment.' In other words, 'not minding even if one becomes attached.' It is about not caring whether attachment exists or not.

The most common reason people become disappointed or give up while engaging in processes like 'becoming free from negative emotions,' as discussed in this text, is not dissimilar. I followed the instructions as described above, yet I still don't feel okay. I practiced the guideline of 'experiencing emotions as they arise without attempting to eliminate them or wishing they would disappear.' Nevertheless, I don't feel better; my mind remains uncomfortable and distressed. So I give up, saying, 'Well, it's not working!'

This text is not about becoming okay, getting better, or having negative emotions disappear to reach a state of well-being. The moment you desire that outcome, you fall back into the familiar trap. Instead, it's about 'being okay with their presence.' Ultimately, it's about 'not minding whether they exist or not.' Recognizing this distinction is crucial.

If we consider the intensity of emotions we experience on a scale from 1 to 10, in the past, we struggled even at levels of 6 or 7. Now, even when experiencing emotions at level 6 or higher, we gradually become more at peace with them. Rather than becoming numb to the emotion, it's about becoming comfortable with 'the very act of experiencing that emotion.' This could also be described as 'willingly feeling' or 'willingly experiencing' the emotion.

Something even more significant is at stake here. The moment when we fail to process primary emotions and consequently experience negative secondary emotions represents both a crisis and an opportunity! This is because we are finally witnessing the true nature of secondary emotions or what is known as the 'second arrow.' In other words, have we finally discovered the 'invisible enemy' that has been tormenting us all along? This is the point where many people stumble or give up midway, passing through without truly understanding what is happening. Let's not miss this insight any longer.

- Don't become hastily disappointed merely because you feel emotions

Secondary emotions are feelings such as disappointment, regret, denial, fear, self-blame, and resignation that emerge when primary emotions aren't properly processed or resolved. 'Ah, why am I feeling this emotion?' I need to process this emotion somehow but I can't. Others say they can do it, so why can't I? It's the feeling of, 'Why must I continue experiencing this emotion as it is?' What is the best approach we can take in this situation?

This is no different from what was discussed previously. We need to stop 'trying to do something' about the negative emotions that arise secondarily. Simply let them be. Feel them without denial or affirmation. Willingly experience them. Simply acknowledge, 'These secondary emotions are arising.' Don't try to eliminate or stop them.

This also requires great courage. At the same time, one is no longer swayed or buried by emotions as in the past. It means not experiencing additional disappointment, worry, anger, helplessness, or sense of guilt simply because the original emotion was felt. Simply accept it, allow it, permit it, acknowledge its existence. Why? Does it not already exist?

When this processing of secondary emotions continues consistently, the intensity of primary emotions gradually subsides. You still experience emotions, but the anxiety or pain that once accompanied them diminishes. It's not about 'emotions disappearing.' That is, it's not about 'becoming numb to feelings.' The absence of feelings cannot be our goal. Unless we are inanimate objects or corpses, why would we, as living beings, desire a state devoid of feelings and emotions? It's about 'feeling but becoming okay with those feelings.' So it's about becoming comfortable with discomfort, willingly accepting and allowing our state of not being okay.

Does this suggest that we should continue to carry our current state of emotional confusion? That is not the case. Of course, it is perfectly acceptable to proceed as you are. This 'acceptability' is also what was mentioned earlier. However, as you begin to properly process emotions as described here, something will gradually subside. What will? The 'unconditional reactions to emotions.' The impulsive, unconscious reactions (secondary emotions) to the emotions we feel (primary emotions) will gradually diminish. And when you begin to feel emotions without being troubled by them, space develops in your mind, enabling you to respond more effectively and practically over time.

Now, let's not be concerned if there are no significant changes along the way. Regardless of what methods we adopt, various situations in our daily lives will continue to arise. Intense emotions, emotional conflicts, arguments, humiliation, disappointment, anxiety, sadness, anger, and other such experiences will recur. Through such experiences, rather than saying 'I really can't do this,' think 'There's still significant inertia remaining. Let me try to stop this more quickly or eliminate it altogether. How can I accomplish this?' and utilize the situation constructively. The more difficult and painful an experience is, the greater becomes our desire to break free from that pattern.

At this point, one might raise the following counterargument.

"Very well. Let's say we permit and experience both primary and secondary emotions. What then?" If negative emotions continue to persist and cannot be addressed, how is this different from before? What purpose do all these attempts and efforts serve? Aren't they futile?

This is not the case. All physiological sensations and feelings naturally dissipate after a certain period once they arise. This is due to the limited lifespan of neural responses.

In other words, whether it's a response through the five senses or an emotional reaction triggered by hormones and thoughts, human physiological and neural responses have a finite lifespan. Some sources estimate this duration to be approximately 90 seconds;

however, in any case, the persistence is likely not as prolonged as one might imagine. In cases of severe physical injury or serious psychological trauma, painful sensations and feelings will naturally persist, necessitating appropriate physical and mental treatment commensurate with the severity of the condition. Unless in exceptional circumstances, generally all sensations and feelings naturally disappear after just a few minutes. Neural activation cannot remain permanent.

Why do so many emotions persist rather than dissipate?

The entity that clings to these emotions is none other than ourselves. In other words, we continuously hold onto emotions that would naturally expire and disappear if simply left alone. Through various forms of stubbornness, thoughts, reminiscences, ruminations, secondary emotions, longings, desires, regrets, needs, beliefs, and so forth. Whether we immerse ourselves in our emotions or deny them, both approaches merely keep us tethered to those emotions. The goal is to cease this pattern of behavior.

- Actively taking the best course of action

Having implemented the psychological coping strategies we have examined thus far, it is now time to proceed to 'practical action-based coping'. Allow yourself to experience emotions without unnecessarily rejecting, suppressing, or attempting to alter them; properly manage secondary emotions as well; and then actively take the best possible actions to overcome, break through, or transform your situation and circumstances!

Acceptance does not mean we should do nothing. We should actively take the actions within our capability. One might question whether there is any need to regulate emotions if we are going to take action anyway. Actions driven by negative reactions to our emotions—specifically, the desire to eliminate those emotions—tend to be impulsive or non-strategic. The results are rarely satisfactory.

While practicing 'emotional regulation'—allowing ourselves to experience emotions as they are—we can simultaneously take actions that change and overcome situations for practical purposes. Then you can act more calmly and with greater composure than when you are buried in or caught up in emotions. Why? Because my purpose or the focus of my consciousness is no longer on 'the emotion itself' but on 'actual resolution'.

What I have discussed thus far primarily concerns 'personal coping' strategies. Structural social problems must be actively addressed and systematically corrected. Typically, these problems extend beyond an individual's efforts and scope, so no matter how diligently one tries to manage their emotions or thoughts, there remains little within their power to change. Therefore, everyone must join forces to dismantle these contradictions. This, too, represents the 'practical behavioral coping' discussed previously.

Finally, there is one more consideration we must address. Remember that not only negative emotions but also 'positive emotions' require processing.

Why would purely positive emotions become problematic? Because whether positive or negative, they are all 'emotions.' That is, they are the same phenomenon, differing only in polarity. If you fail to recognize that positive emotions are also 'emotions to be managed' and unconsciously identify with, assimilate into, and become immersed in them, you will inevitably respond similarly to negative emotions later.

This is not saying to ignore, deny, or avoid enjoying positive emotions. There is no need for that. Rather, it suggests that even while enjoying, relishing, and savoring these emotions, we should remain aware in real-time that they are merely 'emotions'. It is about recognizing that emotions are never the complete truth or the whole picture. This awareness enables us to apply the same perspective to negative emotions later on.

For example, we should be wary not only of aversion toward others but also of indiscriminate worship of them. We should be cautious not only of the inferiority complex that leads us to demean ourselves but also of the unfounded superiority complex. The same context can be applied to sadness and joy, hatred and love, unhappiness and happiness. We must recognize that all these relative emotions are the same 'emotion' mechanism, differing only in their polarity, ultimately forming a unity.

Like negative emotions, positive emotions also produce side effects when one becomes excessively immersed in them. The first is the pain experienced when positive emotions disappear. This can occur when one becomes overly attached to positive emotions. The second is the emergence of unnatural reactions or maladaptive coping mechanisms. When swayed by positive emotions, one can easily respond in exaggerated or contextually inappropriate ways. Of course, positive emotions don't require the same level of caution or concern as negative emotions. One can simply embrace and enjoy them with greater ease. Nevertheless, at their core, they should be treated identically using the methods described above.

To use an analogy, whether it's white paint or black paint, the process of coloring the wall remains the same. This doesn't mean that painting is wrong or should be avoided, but rather that we must understand what the phenomenon of 'painting (emotion)' is, how to approach it, what precautions to take, and what measures are appropriate.

◆ ◆ ◆

Summary

The core of emotion management is not rejecting or attempting to change emotions that have already been experienced. Instead, emotions should be accepted and allowed to exist as they are. Secondary emotions should be approached in the same manner. Emotions naturally dissipate, but they persist because we continue to hold onto them. While managing emotions, it is equally important to take practical actions to improve the underlying situation. Positive emotions should be handled with the same approach, avoiding excessive attachment or immersion.

4.6 Methods for Overcoming the Instinctive Fear of the Unfamiliar

: Beyond 'Fight or Flight' – Mastering Primal Instincts

Humans unconsciously guard against or fear what they do not know or find unfamiliar. A merely neutral 'unknown' almost automatically transforms into a 'fearful thing.' Regarding unfamiliar subjects, it is difficult to remain even indifferent, let alone develop positive feelings or affinity. Such responses require growth experiences, intentional learning, training, and cognitive awakening. However, this natural reaction is not inherently wrong. It is a natural instinctive response possessed by almost all animals. Animals living in the wild naturally need to perceive danger when encountering unfamiliar entities. This is because such entities could be dangerous predators. Perhaps our human ancestors also needed such responses, which would have been beneficial for their survival. However, in civilized life and daily routines, there is no need to remain excessively bound by the 'fear of the unfamiliar.' One must learn to recognize this as an instinctive feeling and develop the capacity to regulate it. This is because such reactions contain unnecessary fear, pain, and conflict.

There is something we must remember: 'difference' is actually a natural phenomenon. In nature, sameness is rather unnatural and rare. 'Similarity,' when examined closely, contains both sameness and difference, thus ultimately constitutes difference. It is merely the result that emerges when we strive to find sameness. In essence, the fundamental state is 'difference.'

- Are all people racists?

As humans, we experience unfamiliarity with various subjects and situations. This occurs even among fellow humans when differences exist in age, gender, social class, or race, and can manifest in social phenomena as well. This applies to different environments, religions, cultures, belief systems, value systems, and moral-ethical frameworks. These fears and aversions constitute the primary causes of conflict between individuals and clashes among groups, societies, and nations in modern civilized society. When negative reactions toward 'different' entities exceed a critical threshold, they escalate into various physical and non-physical conflicts and wars between individuals and groups.

The problem is that a significant portion of these tragedies stems from cognitive errors—mistaking 'instinctive negative feelings arising from unfamiliarity' as facts rather than recognizing actual problems. While each party attributes the cause of conflict to the other, in many cases, these are merely pretexts attached to unconscious inner resistance, fear, and anger that have already formed within.

There is an interesting finding revealed in a neuroscience study related to this topic. A pattern study of the brain reportedly reached a conclusion that could be characterized as 'all people are racists.' In this experiment, subjects whose brain responses were being recorded in real-time via fMRI were shown photographs of people from different races. The results showed that regardless of a person's usual disposition toward racial issues, everyone exhibited activation in certain parts of the limbic system—the brain regions responsible for triggering vigilance, tension, or negative feelings. In other words, racially discriminatory responses can be viewed as everyone's instinctive cautionary reaction to things that are different or unfamiliar.

Is that truly the complete picture? Just because the brain reacts this way, should discrimination, caution, and fear toward all 'unfamiliar or different things,' including racial discrimination, be justified? Certainly not. There is a revealing twist to this experiment: after the initial cautionary response occurred, researchers observed differences in the reaction of the prefrontal cortex, the brain region responsible for reasoning.

In the preliminary investigation, individuals who exhibited racist dispositions showed sustained negative initial reactions in the prefrontal cortex without any significant coping mechanisms, whereas those with fewer racist tendencies demonstrated prefrontal cortex activation that effectively eliminated their instinctive rejection responses. In other words, they counterbalanced their instinctive reactions through the power of rational cognition. Racists, in effect, failed to properly utilize the power of reason. This is likely attributable to personal differences, value systems or belief systems learned from childhood, and socio-cultural differences.

There is an even more significant aspect to consider. In another similar study, researchers examined children who had been exposed to various races from an early age. These children did not even exhibit negative reactions in the limbic system. This was because their consciousness and brain had already become accustomed to different races. In other words, it is possible to perceive oneself and others as familiar entities rather than objects of fear.

This phenomenon is certainly not limited to racial discrimination alone. Doesn't this same process occur across all domains—different genders, ages, feelings, thoughts, belief systems, value systems, ethics, religions, philosophies, political views, cultures, and beyond? We can overcome our instinctive negative reactions to the unknown, the different, and the unfamiliar.

How specifically can we transcend our instinctive negative reactions to the unfamiliar?

When you experience negative feelings about anything, the first step is to 'confront' them. No problem—whether related to emotions, thoughts, people, or situations—can be resolved through avoidance, suppression, or denial. Confrontation can also be described as 'willingly experiencing' what is present. Perceive and recognize the object 'as it is, in its original state' without misunderstanding or distortion. This prevents unnecessary processes from occurring and enables you to respond appropriately.

If a problem persists, it may be because you have not yet grasped and confronted the subject as it truly is. Therefore, one must undergo the process of properly understanding and gaining insight. This is the core process of resolving external problems by addressing negative psychological patterns.

First, acknowledge that differences, unfamiliarity, and ignorance can naturally exist.

This does not mean unconditionally accepting or approving of them. That comes afterward, and whether to accept them or not remains a personal choice. Before that, let us first acknowledge that in any domain, different things, unfamiliar things, and unknown elements can exist. Many problems initially arise because we hold too strongly to the belief that 'such things should never happen.'

Second, recognize that negative feelings and reactions toward different, unfamiliar, or unknown things are 'natural.'

Many people fail to objectify or view their negative reactions objectively, instead becoming immersed in or identified with them. Consequently, they automatically respond only negatively. To break this connection, we must consciously recognize the instinctive negative reactions occurring within ourselves. Sometimes, upon noticing this reaction, one suppresses or avoids the negativity, but as mentioned earlier, suppression or avoidance is never a solution. Eventually, it will inevitably surface.

Most importantly, we must recognize that the negative reactions within us are neither wrong, sinful, nor immature—they are merely instinctive natural responses. This is also the first finding from the fMRI experiment introduced earlier. By healthily feeling and acknowledging these reactions, a significant portion of the negativity resolves itself, allowing us to naturally transition to the next response.

Third, avoid connecting negative reactions to imaginary feelings of 'fear, vigilance, or rejection.'

Once you recognize that your negative reaction is an unnecessary unconscious response, you must intentionally and consciously begin the process of disregarding it. This means first acknowledging and understanding your brain's instinctive reaction, then consciously engaging your brain's rational functions. It's about recognizing that you don't need to act upon the negative reactions generated by your limbic system—simply let them pass. It's understanding 'that's not what's really happening.' Even when it feels real, it is not the truth; thus, we acknowledge the feeling but do not dwell on it.

Taking it a step further, it is even more beneficial to transform these reactions into neutral or positive responses. Naturally, applying this approach to subjects we genuinely dislike or feel aversion toward is never simple. Persistent learning, practice, training, and repetition may be necessary. We possess the mental fortitude to accomplish this. Let us harness this strength. Through this process, we can transcend our instinctive wariness and fear toward people, situations, and all unfamiliar entities.

Summary

Humans instinctively fear the unfamiliar, but this is a primitive response that is no longer necessary in our modern context. According to neurological research, all individuals initially exhibit 'racially discriminatory' responses, but can overcome these through rational cognitive processes. The methods to overcome fear of the unfamiliar are as follows:

1) Acknowledge that differences and unfamiliarity are natural aspects of human experience.

2) Recognize negative emotions as natural psychological responses.

3) Avoid connecting negative reactions with imaginary fears or catastrophic thinking.

Through this approach, we can overcome instinctive fears and respond in more constructive ways.

4.7 To What Extent Am I 'Willingly' Experiencing Myself?

: The Art of Self-Acceptance

We must examine ourselves.
"To what extent am I 'willingly' experiencing myself?"

If that is not the case
We must learn to do so.
It means willingly experiencing myself.

As you may have noticed
The crucial element here is 'willingly.'

This means without unnecessary positive or negative judgments
and without resistance
It means to 'experience' circumstances coolly, dispassionately,
and exactly as they are.

What should not be misunderstood is,
The word 'willingly'
does not suggest that you should do nothing you desire
or remain passive.
If there are actions to take and changes to make
regarding yourself, others, and the world,
do them all. Freely.
And throughout this process,
willingly experience and embrace
yourself, others, and the entire world as well.

It means riding the waves of that experience,
it means traversing through the cave of that experience,
It means traversing the field of that experience,
It means embracing the journey of that experience.

My body, my emotions, my thoughts, my actions,
My environment and circumstances, my very existence.

Regarding everything I experience about myself
Neither being ignorant, nor dismissive,
Neither avoiding, nor suppressing
Without distortion
I first 'willingly' experience, accept,
Acknowledge, feel, and embrace it.

First, let us examine my body.
To what extent am I willingly experiencing my body?

Each person is born with various inherent physical characteristics.
Some individuals are tall while others are short.
Some have fair skin while others have deeper complexions.
Some possess healthy, lustrous hair while others have dry, brittle strands.
Some have larger physical builds while others possess more flexible bodies.
Some excel intellectually while others demonstrate physical dexterity.

This is not a question of superiority or inferiority.
This is simply the manifestation of diversity, freedom, and natural

variation.

Many people
dream of a different physical state than their current body
they envy it while simultaneously turning away from their own
body.

There is no need for this.
Envy only wastes the energy of our lives.
Our ancestors used to say that envying others
'drives away even the fortune you already have.'
This is a wise insight.

Instead of doing that,
since it's the body you were born with, and the body you'll live
with for your entire life,
you simply need to experience it 'willingly.'
Even if you're not 100% satisfied with it
and desire different physical characteristics,
Even so, one can live by experiencing things 'willingly'.
In some cases, this may not be easy,
But that doesn't mean it's impossible.

'To experience willingly' means
Not experiencing something because conditions are favorable,
because you like it, or because you feel superior,
It doesn't mean experiencing it for those reasons.

'To experience willingly' means
Likes and dislikes,
Excellence and inadequacy,

Superiority and inferiority,
Whether something is pleasing or not,
Regardless of all these factors,
It means to experience it nonetheless.
Embracing all conditions and transcending them,
It means to experience life with dignity and resolve.

Two, let us examine my emotions.
Am I properly attending to the emotions I experience?
Am I not dismissing them or treating them as insignificant?
My emotions, moods, and feelings
are 'the voice of life' within me,
yet due to the influence of others and the world,
or through my own conditioning,
am I telling myself 'I shouldn't feel this way'
or am I suppressing or avoiding them
by ignoring or despising myself?

This should not happen.
Regardless of what others and the world say
My emotions and feelings are cosmic truths to me.

What should be noted is that this statement
Being buried in and swept away by my emotions and moods
does not mean they are supreme or the absolute good.
That is rather me, the master of emotions,
becoming a slave to emotions.

Just acknowledge them 'as they are,' feel them,
accept them, and take care of them.

Then my emotions
will bloom by themselves, heal by themselves, and pass by themselves.
In fact, it is impossible to hold onto emotions and prevent them from leaving.
Those emotions that have already passed
We merely grasp or recall them repeatedly.
Therefore, simply let them go and gradually reduce your subsequent reactions.

Emotions are not who I am.
Emotions are merely useful tools
A unity of instruments for navigating life.
I am the master of my emotions,
Whatever emotions are felt and flow through me,
I remain fundamentally intact.

Furthermore,
While I readily accept my positive emotions and moods,
My negative ones
I push away, ignore, or pretend they don't exist
Am I not treating them as such?

Let us refrain from doing that.
Being captured by them, influenced by them
I am not suggesting that you should enter a negative state.
The traumas in my body are also part of me
Just as we nurture and heal physical wounds to recover
The negative emotions and feelings, which are traumas of my mind
Are also integral parts of myself

Like physical traumas, let us acknowledge them, accept them,
Nurture them with care and facilitate their healing.

Rather than identifying ourselves with our emotions
Instead of being captured by or submerged in emotions
As the master of your mind, when you properly notice, deeply feel,
compassionately embrace, and fully acknowledge your emotions,
Emotions will pass through and resolve themselves.

Three, let's observe our thoughts.
To what extent am I
willingly experiencing my own thoughts?

Throughout our waking hours
and even in this moment as you read these words,
thoughts continuously arise and pass away.
This is almost an automatic function of the brain.
Rather than me controlling my thoughts,
thoughts spontaneously emerge
and pass across the screen of my consciousness.

To willingly experience our thoughts means,
First, to truly acknowledge our own thoughts.
To recognize what we are thinking.
Next, it means discerning the true nature of thoughts.
That I am the owner of my thoughts, not that thoughts define who
I am.
That thoughts are merely tools for myself and for life.

So whatever thoughts arise and pass,
Without denying them or becoming absorbed in them,

I can healthily and confidently
Willingly experience all my thoughts.

Therefore,
Not automatically reacting as thoughts arise,
But rather utilizing and employing those thoughts.

If the thought is useful and necessary, use it well,
If it arises but serves little purpose,
Simply let it flow away.
Then the thought passes.
If I don't cling to it, it simply passes by.

Of course, unnecessary thoughts may continue to resurface.
When this happens, acknowledge it with 'Ah, it's appearing again'
And release it without attaching negative or positive emotions.
Saying, 'It was nice to meet you again. Take care~'.

Because that thought is not me.

The more willingly I experience my thoughts like this,
I gradually become the master of my thoughts and use them
rather than being used by them.

Fourth, let's examine my actions, environment, and situation.
We need only to effectively utilize one fundamental principle.
It is 'the distinction between my work and God's work.'

We worry excessively about the meaning and consequences
of our actions.
Whether we are truly doing well,

Whether what we do has meaning,
Whether the results will be favorable, and so forth.

The same applies to the people and situations around us.
The reactions of others,
The emotions, thoughts, and actions of others
I yearn for them to conform to my wishes.

I also want the other environments and situations surrounding me
To be arranged and proceed
As closely as possible to what I desire.

However, we must clearly distinguish between 'my business' and
What is not my business, namely 'God's business'.
We must make a clear distinction between these domains.

The 'God's business' referred to here
Is not referring to anything religious.
It refers to all matters that are not 'my business.'

About the consequences of actions, others, environment, and situations.
We treat things that are not our business,
Even things that we cannot control,
Presumptuously mistaking them as 'our business.'
We become restless and don't know what to do.

When we begin to treat God's business
As our own and strive to manage it,
Our suffering begins.

I only need to attend to 'my business,'
Only what I can actually do,
And simply do my best at it.
Then 'God's business' is
Surrender it to the divine.
The divine also needs purpose
So give your burdens over.

Then all matters that are not my responsibility
Will flow according to their natural course.
Let us always remember this wisdom of life.

Finally, let us examine my existentiality.
My feelings, thoughts, and actions that we've explored earlier,
Along with the sum of everything beyond these,
Constitute my complete existentiality.

Am I willingly experiencing my entire existentiality?
Or do I selectively accept certain parts
While denying other aspects of myself
Are you avoiding, ignoring, and pretending it doesn't exist?

If such things exist
Now let's willingly experience each one
Let's conquer them one by one.

Of course, if there are things that need to be changed in others
and the world
Let's also do everything in our power to change them.
This is a right that we all inherently possess
and also a responsibility.

Active responses and actions are also
included in the process of willing experience.

At the same time
Regardless of others and the world
I am the entirety of myself
Let us live a life where we willingly embrace our experiences.

And
Finally
Others and even the world itself
Willingly embrace
Willingly let go.

◆ ◆ ◆

Summary

Willingly experiencing oneself is the essence of self-acceptance. This means experiencing oneself as one is, without judgment. This process encompasses all aspects of oneself: body, emotions, thoughts, behaviors, and environment. The crucial element is experiencing 'willingly,' which means accepting all conditions regardless of whether we like them or not. It is also important to distinguish between your own work and 'God's work,' avoiding unnecessary worry about things beyond your control. Ultimately, by willingly experiencing and accepting your entire existence, you can live a more abundant life.

Chapter 5: For Those Who Aspire to Be Protagonists in Their Relationships

5.1 A Message to Those Who Believe They Are Not Protagonists

5.2 Do Not Devalue Yourself

5.3 How to Handle 'Opposing Viewpoints' That Distress You

5.4 Cease Being a 'Pushover'

5.5 Cultivate Horizontal Love, Not Vertical Dependency

5.6 Empathy Does Not Require Becoming an Emotional Dumping Ground

5.7 Apologies: For Myself, For Others, For Everyone

5.8 Rediscovering Myself Through My Other Self

5.9 You and I are neither 'two separate entities' nor simply 'one'. We are 'Duality within unity'

5.10 Two Truths (N Truths - N Ranges from 0 to Infinity)

5.1 A Message to Those Who Believe They Are Not Protagonists

: Breaking the Protagonist Myth - Shifting Focus from Being the Protagonist to Becoming the Director of Your Life

When a performer in a magnificent concert hall
Playing the beautiful cello performance.
The audience is absorbed in appreciating the performance.

In this situation
Who is the protagonist?

No one is the protagonist.
Yet simultaneously, everyone is the protagonist.

If necessary, we determine a protagonist.
But if not particularly necessary, we refrain from doing so.
If needed, I will become the protagonist.
If not needed, I will allow another to be the protagonist.
Therefore, the protagonist sometimes exists and sometimes does not,
It is merely a construct of unity that can exist or not exist.

Whether performer, audience, staff, or anyone else
Regardless of the limitation or constraint called 'protagonist',
Whether one considers oneself the protagonist or not
One can exist confidently and proudly.

The same applies to relationships, daily life, and work.

We are,
Beyond being the protagonist or not,
The masters of all those settings.

In relationships, work, and daily life, we constantly evaluate who is more important, who is more central, who is more meaningful, and so on. Sometimes we do this openly and sometimes privately in our minds. At times consciously, at other times unconsciously.

Such distinctions are possible even in intimate relationships between couples or among a few friends, let alone in larger groups. It is a kind of 'comparative mindset.' Or it is also an act that determines a person's meaning or value.

No one is exempt from the habit of comparison. Even a 'protagonist' figure who is envied by all will, when entering a group of similar individuals, begin analyzing who the new protagonist is and whether they themselves can claim that role. The 'suicide crisis among elite American university students' that has made headlines follows this same pattern. When individuals who were regarded as exceptional in their respective environments gather in one place, they instinctively measure themselves against others to identify the new protagonist. Those who conclude it isn't them may ultimately choose death, overwhelmed by the pressure and stress related to their abilities, position, and very existence.

In this way, 'determining life's protagonist and making comparisons' is a mental game that occurs everywhere.

Let us reflect on this carefully.

What exactly are these constructs of 'protagonist' and 'non-protagonist'?

Do they truly possess actual meaning and value?

Someone might contend: I have little interest in being the

protagonist in any relationship, group, or situation. However, the term 'protagonist' here serves as a symbolic expression. To elaborate, it refers to 'a person of greater meaning, greater importance, greater value, or greater respect,' and so forth. Few people refrain from scrutinizing matters to this degree.

Conversely, one might ask: What's wrong with being a bit critical? Isn't such a mindset simply human nature? Indeed, it could be entirely natural. The problem arises when this mindset causes psychological suffering. If one has no worries, no hardships, and no complaints, what problem could possibly exist? However, if one is preoccupied with becoming the protagonist, if the mind is troubled, and if disruptive events occur, then there is a genuine need to address the problem.

To present the answer upfront, it is this.

At any moment in life, in any situation, there is no such thing as a protagonist.

Therefore, everything is also a protagonist.

Regardless of such concepts, we always exist with dignity and integrity.

It's not saying 'there is no protagonist,' but rather that the very concept of 'protagonist' doesn't exist. It means we don't concern ourselves with such concepts. It means we don't concern ourselves with it, nor are we influenced by it. In other words, it refers to transcending both the term 'protagonist'—which distinguishes and gives special status to people considered more important, meaningful, or valuable—and the 'act of distinction itself' that assigns such labels. It is recognizing that this is merely done according to necessity and is not absolute. Whether there is someone who plays the role of the protagonist or not is completely unimportant. If necessary, anyone can and should assume this role.

You might ask, what does this mean when there are clearly more active people, more knowledgeable people, more proactive people, and more important people? Yes, such people do exist. However, specifically labeling them as 'protagonists' has nothing to do with who they actually are. This is equally true in reverse for those who are not protagonists. Without protagonists, non-protagonists cannot exist. Whether such limitations, parameters, or restrictions exist or not, we exist proudly and confidently regardless of them.

Whether one performs slightly better or worse than others, that's simply how it is—there's no need to feel additionally boastful or intimidated because of it.

What we actually struggle with is not the question of who the protagonist is, but rather the feeling and thought that 'I am not the protagonist'—meaning 'I am nothing special.' No one is exempt from this psychological pattern. Because someone who is the protagonist in one place often becomes insignificant in another. Particularly when one repeatedly finds themselves as 'not the protagonist—essentially insignificant' in places where they have relationships and belong, they experience depression, psychological withdrawal, self-loathing, self-deprecation, self-disappointment, helplessness, feelings of incompetence, and loneliness.

For instance, among celebrities, there are those who occasionally suffer from symptoms of panic disorder. This is a symptom that occurs when one's sense of self becomes excessively inflated when receiving public adoration, then collapses dramatically when that adulation ceases. Of course, ordinary individuals can also experience similar phenomena in their own circumstances. Sometimes, this occurs due to anxiety such as, 'What if they discover my true incompetent self after recognizing me like this now?'

While this is an issue that working adults face, recently children have also become victims of this negative psychological state. According to research, children in Korean society suffer from 'negative self-perception' due to comparison with others and competition at significantly higher rates than children in other countries. They are enduring unnecessary psychological distress.

Because each person has different abilities, preferences, and dispositions, we may experience being a 'less important person' in various situations. The same applies to experiences of being a 'more important person.' In itself, this is not problematic. What creates a problem where none exists is the conscious categorization, distinction, and comparison between being a 'protagonist, more important, meaningful person' versus 'someone who is not.'

To use an analogy, it's as if I'm standing on a blank white floor, when suddenly I or someone else draws a circle around me, after which I convince myself that I'm trapped within it. It refers to the original concept of being a 'protagonist,' and sometimes a 'non-protagonist.' If it's unnecessary, one could simply step outside the circle, yet they find themselves unable to do so. It's not that they cannot exit, but rather that 'they merely believe they cannot leave.' Moreover, it isn't even necessary to eliminate the circle completely. One simply needs to understand that the presence of the circle is inconsequential. Rather, one utilizes the circle according to their needs.

There is a famous experiment known as the 'glass jar experiment.' A fly is placed inside a glass jar, and the opening is sealed with a glass plate. The fly attempts to exit several times, but repeatedly collides with the glass panel. Eventually, the fly resigns itself to circling inside the glass jar. Then, the glass panel is removed. Now the entrance is open, but the fly still only approaches where the glass panel once was before flying back into the jar, unable to escape.

This is not only an actual experiment but also a metaphor in itself. It illustrates the 'mental glass panel' where one believes 'I cannot escape' rather than actually being physically confined.

- Again, who is the protagonist?

Let's return to the initial cello performance scene.

Who is the protagonist?

If it is a critically important concert for the performer, then designate them as the protagonist. If it is a birthday party, wedding reception, or an event for a special audience, then that individual or the audience becomes the protagonist. As before, this can be determined and applied according to the situation and necessity.

There is no need to deny, reject, or claim that the concept of a protagonist does not exist. If necessary, create and utilize that framework, but when unnecessary, recognize that 'it is merely a construct.' The more clearly we perceive, the more unnecessary reactions gradually fade away.

On the other hand, another thought occurs to me.

Would a performance have meaning without an audience? If there were no performer, would the audience have reason to be present? The same applies to event staff. What about the instruments? Most importantly, what if there were no performance sound? The concert is the culmination of all these elements harmonizing together. No element can exist independently. Categorizing them as performers, audience, staff, instruments, and so forth is merely a distinction of convenience. All are simultaneously necessary. In essence, the distinction between protagonist and non-protagonist is fundamentally meaningless.

In a sense, every event in our lives represents a new cello performance. Romantic relationships, family, friends, gatherings, school, company, various communities—and all the phenomena, relationships, and events that occur within them—let us experience them confidently and willingly as they truly are. Let us not become confined by unnecessary constructs, meaningless boundaries, or imaginary barriers. Let us recognize that even if these limitations appear to exist, they need not constrain us.

We are the masters who create and draw all these settings and circles, not beings destined to be trapped within them. Being trapped is, in fact, impossible—even within the construct of being a 'protagonist.'

◆ ◆ ◆

Summary

The concept of 'protagonist' has no real meaning in authentic existence. There is no need to designate someone as a protagonist in every situation; we should only do so when genuinely necessary. What truly matters is not whether one is a protagonist, but that every person can exist confidently and proudly in their own unique role. We are the masters of these roles and must break free from unnecessary comparison and distinction. Every aspect of life is like playing a new cello piece, where all elements are simultaneously necessary and important. Therefore, as creators of these settings and boundaries, we should experience our lives freely and confidently.

5.2 Do Not Devalue Yourself

: The Art of Self-Respect - Body, Emotion, and Thought

If you feel ignored by someone or by the people you usually associate with, there is something you should examine first.

Typically in such cases, one attributes blame to others or the situation. From my perspective, I believe I'm thinking, expressing, and behaving appropriately, yet others and my environment are dismissing me.

The responsibility for everything related to 'me' is precisely 50-50. This means half the responsibility is mine and half belongs to external factors. These two aspects are organically connected, so when one changes, the other inevitably transforms as well. (In this sense, one could also frame it as 100% my responsibility.)

If you feel that in daily life you receive disrespect and dismissal from others rather than respect and mature treatment, the cause is quite simple.

It is because you are first giving yourself away at a 'cheap price' continuously.

Is that too obvious an answer? The literal content may be, but the way of examining it is different. There are various ways in which we habitually offer ourselves 'cheaply' to others and the world. Let's consider roughly three domains: body, emotion, and thought. Sometimes all three occur simultaneously, while at other times only one manifests.

Surrendering one's body means, literally, permitting others to use one's physical self as they wish. Of course, this does not imply allowing others to inappropriately touch or molest one's body. It refers to all activities and actions that involve physically engaging one's body throughout life.

Surrendering one's emotions means devaluing one's feelings and reactions. Treating them as worthless. By oneself. Consequently, others tend to disregard or ignore the emotional dimensions of my being. Why would others value something that its owner considers worthless?

This is not suggesting that you become a selfish individual who is faithful only to their own emotions and values them exclusively. Rather, it means you must first acknowledge that your emotions are vital elements and companions in life—you must feel them deeply, recognize them accurately, express them effectively, and process them appropriately.

If you don't attend to your own emotions first, others will naturally either remain unaware or make assumptions about them. What can we do? None of us yet possesses telepathic abilities. Thus, others unintentionally disregard us and our emotions, treating them as if they were of little value.

Finally, surrendering your thoughts means failing to express them objectively because you've become immersed in or attached to your own thoughts, opinions, or perspectives. Therefore, one must know how to properly express and present oneself at one's 'proper value' as an 'objective element' that will benefit both oneself and others in unity.

This is easily understood through a simple example. For instance, A wants to climb a mountain. B lives facing the mountain. C lives on the left side of the mountain, while I live behind it. Now B, C, and I each provide different information about 'the location of the mountain' with the intention of helping A. If A is wise, they will be able to accurately determine the mountain's location by listening to all three perspectives. If I were to excessively prioritize B or C's thoughts over my own and fail to properly express my perspective, this could actually create problems. My thoughts deserve to be expressed or presented at their full value as 'objective elements' that can benefit others. This serves both myself and those around me.

Let us begin by assigning proper value to our bodies, emotions, and thoughts, then present them at their true worth to others and the world. Similarly, let us pay others the full value they deserve.

Summary

The habit of undervaluing oneself can manifest in three domains: physical, emotional, and cognitive. This includes treating your body carelessly, neglecting your emotions, or failing to properly express your thoughts. It is important to properly perceive and express your own intrinsic worth. This does not mean becoming selfish, but rather valuing all aspects of yourself and expressing them appropriately. Others will respect you to the extent that you respect yourself. Additionally, you must equally acknowledge the value of others.

5.3 How to Handle 'Opposing Viewpoints' That Distress You

: The Art of Responding, Not Reacting

Opposition is always bitter. How should I react and respond when someone opposes my views, thoughts, or expressions? Even between the closest friends, a single opposing opinion can cause a dispute, and my opposing view might traumatize the other person, potentially ending the relationship.

These days, there are many opportunities to express our opinions through social media and other platforms, and consequently, just as many opportunities to receive reactions to them. Sometimes debates arise with opposing viewpoints that can seem quite 'intense' to those involved. Of course, this happens in offline interactions as well.

When confronted with opposing opinions, the primary reaction is a 'physiological response'—a physical reaction within the body. This typically manifests as a tension response, specifically a sympathetic nervous system activation. The degree and intensity of these reactions vary according to each person's innate physiological mechanisms. One might experience sudden tensing of muscles throughout the body, an indescribable discomfort in the lower abdomen, or heart palpitations. The face may also flush with blood, creating a sensation of heat. Beyond these physiological reactions, feelings of discomfort, resentment, and anger will naturally arise.

All of these responses are entirely natural. This isn't because I'm narrow-minded, weak-hearted, arrogant, immature, or naive. These are sensations that any living being would naturally experience.

Of course, through dedicated training or psychological insight, these initial physiological and psychological responses may gradually diminish over time, but this needn't be our primary objective. Even a single-celled organism like an amoeba reacts when it collides with something. 'Reaction' is entirely natural; its absence would be the anomaly.

There is neuroscientific evidence to support this as well. The most recent studies indicate that the brain regions responding to psychological obstacles are identical to those responding to physical obstacles. This means that the brain areas activated when a person encounters a physical obstacle while walking are the same areas that respond when facing abstract and psychological threats, opposition, or obstacles related to religion, ideology, or one's social group.

The key lies in the secondary response. In other words, our secondary responses to physiological and psychological reactions are more significant. How do we respond to the natural friction and resistance that emerges when our thoughts advance and collide with other thoughts?

The most problematic secondary response is the secondary 'emotional reaction.' Primary physiological responses are pure signals without inherent positive or negative qualities, yet we tend to interpret and experience these signals negatively (particularly in cases of opposing reactions). These 'negative interpretations and feelings' become our Secondary response.

The Primary response is, literally, our initial pure reaction. This occurs because it emerges when two entities moving in different directions collide. Simply accept, acknowledge, affirm, and embrace it exactly as it is and as it feels. And do not concern yourself with the reaction itself. Instead, simply 'utilize' it effectively. Like an amoeba, either climb over what stands before you, circumvent it, or turn in the opposite direction. That is the correct approach.

Unlike the inevitable primary response, the secondary response has room for adjustment. In other words, there is potential for improvement depending on our efforts. If that still doesn't work, one can try again at the tertiary or quaternary response level.

Typically, problems arise when we attempt to control the inevitable primary response or when we refuse to accept and psychologically acknowledge it. These are all secondary responses. We must become aware of this pattern. In essence, the secondary response is the very act of refusing to acknowledge the naturalness of the primary response. It encompasses all reactions that follow when we believe the primary response 'must be dealt with.' This proceeds quite subtly, which is why most people fail to notice it.

The most common secondary response to opposing opinions is negative feelings about oneself: 'Am I easy to push around? Do I appear insignificant? What did I do wrong? What do they take me for? Don't they recognize who I am?' among various others. Opposition, conflict, and resistance actually have nothing to do with the 'self'. It is merely a collision between 'a fragment of my thought' and another 'fragment of thought'. Of course, there is a process of identification between myself and the thought as the subject who harbors and expresses that thought, but regardless of that relationship, the thought itself is not my true self. Many people associate opposing opinions not with their 'thoughts' but with their 'sense of self,' and thus escalate the situation. This is what leads them into confusion.

To use an analogy, imagine I throw a ball and someone else's thrown ball collides with mine. In unexpected situations like this, one might become angry or upset. Nevertheless, fundamentally the ball is the ball, and I am I. There might be the inconvenience of having to return the ball, but 'I who threw the ball' am essentially not directly connected to that collision.

Another secondary response is the negative feeling towards the other person. 'What's with that person? Why does he hate me? Why is he so negative? Why is his thinking so short-sighted? Why is his thinking so strange?' 'Fine, I'll get revenge too, see you later, you're finished' and various other thoughts.

To use another analogy, the thoughts expressed by another person are like a ball they have thrown. Just as that person is not the ball itself, that person's thoughts are not the person. We typically attack, hate, or become angry at 'that person.' And then we fall into confusion.

Of course, in some cases, matters don't end with merely expressing an opinion, and serious consequences may follow. In such situations, one should take active and appropriate measures suited to the circumstances. Let us not misunderstand—this does not mean we should do nothing and remain passive. This text explores how to take optimal actions while cultivating the most beneficial mindset.

Most opposing viewpoints we encounter in daily life are merely 'differences in perspective.' Rarely do new problematic situations arise simply because of differing viewpoints. Yet we fail to permit and accept even these 'differences in thinking.' In doing so, we become a kind of 'mental dictator.' If I possessed power, I might desire to ruthlessly eliminate or delete any differing thoughts. In the 'realm of thoughts' within my mind, I have already become a dictator. Of course, as long as I don't express this externally, no harm is done, but I become distressed internally.

Now, as we have examined thus far, there are two key points in responding to opposing opinions.

First, accept, understand, and recognize the primary response that arises from conflict and resistance as a natural phenomenon. By doing so, one avoids progressing to unnecessary subsequent responses.

Second, properly address the secondary response, which comprises additional interpretations and feelings about the primary response. Willingly experience these as they arise. In other words, it is about cultivating mindful detachment. Allow reactions to flow and pass naturally, regardless of whether they manifest, without concern. Note that this is not about directly controlling, changing, or eliminating the secondary response. Such intentions themselves constitute secondary responses. The key is to view unaddressed, or uncontrolled, secondary responses as naturally as one would view primary responses. While managing your mind in this way, simply complete all the external tasks that need to be done.

◆ ◆ ◆

Summary

There are two key points in dealing with opposing opinions. First, accept and understand the natural physiological responses caused by conflict and resistance. This prevents unnecessary subsequent reactions. Second, properly manage secondary responses, which are additional interpretations and emotions that arise from primary responses. It is important to accept secondary reactions as they are and to develop indifference toward them. Uncontrolled secondary reactions should be viewed as natural as primary reactions. Simultaneously, external behaviors should be addressed according to necessity. This approach helps reduce unnecessary conflict and stress caused by opposing viewpoints.

5.4 Cease Being a 'Pushover'

: Beyond the Frame - Cultivating Independence and Self-Confidence

In some respects, life is an endless war of frame-setting. Here, 'frame' can be understood as a 'cognitive framework'. It is a struggle about whether one can capture and confine others within one's own frame or how free one can remain from others' frames.

Frames exist in all domains of life. This encompasses everything from our self-image to our environment, our value, abilities and existentiality, our value system, perspectives on work, relationships and life, as well as various moral, ethical, religious, philosophical, and scientific viewpoints. In a word, it refers to 'a specific perspective across all domains.'

Theoretically, winning a frame war is simple. One must avoid being drawn into the opponent's strategy of co-option. In other words, don't become trapped within it. Easier said than done. But in reality, we inevitably become entangled with people and situations. Almost as if under some magical spell.

Why does this happen? It occurs because we overlook the following crucial fact.

A frame is not an 'absolute truth.' It is merely a 'cognitive framework.'

The frames presented by others and society are merely 'their frameworks,' not absolute truths. Of course, depending on the situation, some frames may be closer to facts or more practical and meaningful than others. Additionally, we should not reject all external frames simply because they come from outside sources. If a certain frame is objectively more accurate or advantageous than mine in terms of utility, willingly accepting and utilizing it would benefit me as well.

The problem arises when that is not the case. Often, I unknowingly become confined within frames that are asserted or imposed from external sources, even when they are not at all beneficial to me, are inaccurate, or even entirely wrong. No, the expression 'confined' is not quite appropriate. The reality is that 'I myself voluntarily enter into that frame.'

There is a very subtle process underlying this phenomenon. It stems from human conversational habits; we almost automatically accept what others say as fact and engage in dialogue accordingly. It is true that this approach facilitates smooth and effective conversation. However, strictly speaking, this is a 'construct' we have created ourselves. We have chosen to operate this way for the convenience of conversation and communication. At some point, we forget that this is our own choice and begin to believe that 'what others say is inherently important, absolute, and factual.' This is an unconscious automatic response.

The problem is that we do this inadvertently even when there is no need to do so.

We often continue to regard the frames imposed by others as important and absolute, frequently thinking or conversing within these frames even when there is no necessity to do so. This occurs because it has already become habitual and feels natural to us. However, if we mechanically follow this pattern, we eventually find ourselves trapped in frames presented by others even when they are unnecessary. We become confined. This happens not because the other person's frame is powerful or special, but because we 'have chosen to do so ourselves.' Recognizing this aspect is most crucial.

This is also a kind of 'evolutionary shortcut.' This occurs because we have a psychological tendency to comfortably utilize the adequate frame presented by others rather than expending effort to create our own. It is a form of efficiency. However, in other cases, we inevitably encounter frames that are unnecessary or harmful to us. If we blindly accept such frames merely for comfort, adverse effects will eventually emerge.

- Evaluating the utility of another person's frame

How we handle a presented frame is, in many ways, a matter of pure choice. Usually, this mechanism occurs unconsciously. That is why we must bring it into consciousness. When we raise something to consciousness, we can actively discern which choices are wiser and more useful. This is precisely the effect of 'conscious integration of the unconscious.'

Whenever we encounter external frames, we should always consider the following two principles.

1. If it serves my needs, I respond by centering my approach on the other person's frame. It involves adjusting our thoughts, reactions, and behaviors to align with these circumstances.

2. If something is unnecessary for me, I deliberately avoid reacting within the other person's frame. Instead, I either remain detached or propose an alternative frame.

By mindfully attending to these two aspects alone, we can significantly reduce the risk of becoming an 'easy person'—someone who unwittingly becomes entangled in others' words or intentions in daily life.

Treating the other person's statements and their frame as important, and centering the conversation around them as described in point 1, is by no means incorrect behavior. This is the evolutionary outcome that humans have developed through communication. It is a highly useful and wise approach. Therefore, engaging in this practice is highly beneficial. Moreover, in today's era where empathy is increasingly important, we must further develop such capabilities. Doing so enables us to better understand others and our environment, allowing for more effective responses.

However, this alone is insufficient. While in the past we may have relied solely on this approach, henceforth, as suggested in point 2, let us either disregard unnecessary frames or propose alternative ones. This is not about engaging in battles of pride or power struggles. Rather, it is an effort to create a more efficient and effective situation for both myself and the other person.

Not all frames presented to me are correct or appropriate. Naturally, one must rigorously examine accuracy, validity, rationality, and appropriateness. No matter how much we have evolved to value and focus on others' words, we must adapt their application according to the specific situation.

With a little mindfulness, you can simultaneously monitor these two aspects and respond appropriately. Of course, this may not be easy. If past patterns are deeply ingrained, you will repeatedly find yourself trapped in the other person's frame, even when you're fully aware of what's happening. However, the key is to continue your efforts without succumbing to disappointment or frustration. It's about maintaining awareness of both the utilization and rejection of frames simultaneously. It's consciously recognizing which of these two options you are choosing for yourself. Then it gradually becomes imprinted in your consciousness and you become able to apply it in actual conversations. And from a certain point, these two aspects begin to be clearly distinguished in real time. They become visible. You can calmly assess 'whether this frame is acceptable' without being mindlessly entangled in the other person's frame. To the extent that you can perceive this, you can make active choices.

Observing yourself calmly examining the utility of external frames and deliberately choosing whether to engage with them, rather than helplessly falling into them, will be a pleasurable experience that words cannot adequately describe.

- Dogs chase thrown stones, but lions attack the person who threw them.

Another way to avoid easily falling into someone else's frame and not becoming an easy target is to confront 'the person who spoke' rather than engaging with the content of the frame itself. The most famous metaphor for this concept is as follows.

'When a stone is thrown, a dog chases the stone, but a lion attacks the person who threw it.'

Let's consider an example. Someone might throw a negative frame about your appearance or body—claiming you're ugly or overweight. Or they might label you as incompetent. Then, most often, we begin to chase after the 'stone' that has been thrown. Our feelings, thoughts, and reactions immediately become entangled in the frame—that is, in the content of those words.

As a result, we exhibit two types of reactions. The first reaction is becoming fully conscious of the ugliness or incompetence the other person has attributed to us, focusing all our attention on it and absorbing the negative impact entirely. The second reaction is becoming angry while refuting or resisting those words. Whether we express it outwardly or suppress it inwardly, both reactions are like a dog diligently chasing after that thrown stone. In essence, we voluntarily enter the prison of that frame. Perhaps the person who threw the stone is watching this reaction with a satisfied smile.

The primary reason we chase 'the thrown stone' is because we are too entangled with our self-image within that particular frame. We place our attention and focus solely on ourselves. That is precisely why we remain stuck. This does not mean that you should disregard yourself or consider yourself unimportant. We should pay attention to ourselves more than anyone else and value our own importance. The problem arises when we do this even when unnecessary. One should only do so when needed, or simply maintain it as an underlying assumption. In fact, when not particularly necessary, maintaining a certain detachment toward yourself can be more effective. This allows you to remain unaffected by whatever frame others might impose upon you. This is because there is no 'self' that can be caught in the frame. Though not easy, this method, when executed properly, is the most powerful approach.

Then, what does it mean to 'pounce on the person who threw the stone' like a lion?

It means shifting the focus of attention to the speaker themselves rather than paying attention to their words or frame. This typically takes the form of questions or inquiries.

'Why is this person saying such things to me?'

'I wonder what underlying motives they have?'

'Judging by how carelessly they speak, their character must not be fully developed.'

'Could they have insecurities about their appearance?'

In this situation, being curious about why the other person is saying such things is not about assigning blame or finding fault, but rather to redirect the focus of attention to 'the person themselves.' It's about cultivating genuine curiosity. Even if you aren't curious, the strategy is to confront the person who created the frame rather than engaging with the words (frame) they've presented. Like a lion, with a 'Roar~!' The other person will likely be startled by this approach. 'I thought I was pursuing a stone, but suddenly it attacked me!'

Rather than merely harboring curiosity internally, you can actually pose questions directly. When someone speaks negatively to me, instead of becoming trapped in their words or internalizing them, I can adopt a serious demeanor and redirect questions back to that person.

"By the way, why would you say something like that? Has someone told you that you are unattractive (or incompetent)?"

"I didn't think you were the type of person who would speak so carelessly, which is disappointing. Perhaps my judgment was incorrect."

"Are you perhaps someone who judges people based on appearance?"

"How would you feel if someone carelessly made such remarks to you?"

There are many other questions one could ask in this situation.

When you focus on the person rather than the frame like this, several advantages emerge. One advantage is that your thoughts are no longer entangled in unnecessary frames. You no longer get drawn into pointless games. The second is that you can provide a subtle warning to the person who created the unnecessary frame. This is also a case of me applying reverse framing. By doing so, I prevent the other person's frame from taking effect. Mentioning the other person or asking counter-questions is one of the most effective methods to avoid falling into the other person's frame.

- Returning the Frame

The third method to free yourself from others' framing is

'returning the frame'.

When someone tries to impose a frame on you, don't feel compelled to answer within that frame. No one has an obligation to think and respond only within a frame simply because they received a question or had such a frame imposed on them. Therefore, let's return that frame back to the other person so they can come to their senses. We are simply redirecting it back to its source. At times, this is the most appropriate response and treatment. The following examples will illustrate this clearly.

To someone who unnecessarily demeans another person's appearance: "Your own appearance isn't particularly impressive either."

To someone who dismisses others' abilities: "I doubt you could perform even this well yourself."

To someone who carelessly criticizes another's thoughts: "Your own thoughts aren't particularly noteworthy either."

To someone who evaluates others carelessly, "The way you evaluate others so casually doesn't earn a favorable assessment from me."

To someone who discriminates unreasonably, "I see you appreciate this kind of discrimination." "How would you feel if you were subjected to such discrimination yourself?"

As some of you may have already noticed, all the content presented here strictly comprises techniques for 'healthy defense.' There is no reason to unnecessarily make others fall into our frame or attack them—at least not unless it's absolutely necessary. Many people also refrain from attacking others first or attempting to impose their views.

The problem is that occasionally, some people do behave this way. In such instances, you can respond appropriately by applying the perspectives and techniques discussed in this text. The key is neither to attack first nor to passively accept victimization. Avoid becoming unnecessarily 'vulnerable' to others. This is the purpose of this text.

- When necessary, be willing to step outside your own frame

There is a crucial point that should not be overlooked at this juncture. My frame is also merely one cognitive framework that I possess. We must recognize this. Whether mine or belonging to others, no frame represents absolute truth or singular reality. It benefits me to use frames appropriately and effectively when needed, but to flexibly discard them when they no longer serve a purpose. In other words, whether mine or others', a frame is merely a 'cognitive framework'—never an absolute fact, singular truth, or inevitable reality. Recognizing this distinction clearly is essential.

If you reject others' frames while treating your own as absolute, you remain trapped in the belief that 'frames represent absolute truth.' Though I may hold my own frame as special, it is, ultimately, still just a frame. A paint-stained left hand can never clean the paint from the right hand. Both hands must be cleansed. Frames are much like this paint.

Neither 'the frame is me' nor 'the frame is not me' captures the complete truth. It's simply about effectively utilizing the phenomenon of 'identification with frames.' By recognizing the true nature of this phenomenon, we can employ it when necessary and set it aside when it isn't.

First, I must liberate myself, and then extend that freedom to others. Neither I nor others should become imprisoned in self-created frames; rather, we should actively master and utilize any frame. This is truly worthy of becoming our purpose. Reverse questioning and reverse framing only have genuine value when they are employed as means to achieve such purposes. Always remember that the goal is not to trap yourself or others in another frame, but rather to collectively enjoy 'freedom from unnecessary frames'.

◆ ◆ ◆

Summary

This section explains methods to avoid becoming easily entangled in 'frames' (mindsets). The key strategies are as follows:

1) Evaluate the usefulness of external frames, and when unnecessary, either disregard them or propose alternative frames.

2) Focus on the person who presented the frame rather than the content of the frame.

3) Return unnecessary frames to their source.

Also, recognize that your own frames are not absolute truths, and you should be able to freely use or discard them as needed. This approach allows you to escape unnecessary frames and engage in more liberated and independent thinking.

5.5 Horizontal Love, Not Vertical Dependence

: Love vs. dependency - Forming relationships that empower

"Moses, Jesus Christ, Muhammad, Lama, Buddha. None of them received sufficient earthly love.

"That cannot be true. All of them have hundreds of thousands, even millions of worshippers to this day?

"To worship means to depend. Dependency does not equate to love. Dependency merely strips away the 'power of thought'—a faculty unique to humans. When a person depends on someone, they degrade and betray themselves, and paradoxically, distance themselves from the very object of their dependency.

This is a passage from a book I read recently.

The text above uses the word 'worship,' but in ordinary relationships, this could be characterized as 'dependency.' What we should share is not dependency but love. Even Jesus and Buddha desired to share love with people, not adoration. They likely rejected all worship—that is, dependency—directed toward them personally. Many such examples can be found in Buddhist scriptures and the Bible. This is because we have come to understand that one-sided dependency only impedes genuine exchange and love between individuals.

Let us redirect our focus inward, toward ourselves. Many of us claim to love another person when, in reality, we are merely dependent on them. The more elements of dependency present in a relationship, the more difficult it becomes for both ourselves and the other person. The method to distinguish between dependency and love is simple. Vertical dependency creates tension within us, while horizontal love offers the gifts of comfort and freedom.

Even when I recognize my dependency on someone, breaking free from that pattern is not easy. This is because it triggers fears within my inner self. The fear of no longer having someone to depend on. At such times, I may wonder whether leaving the relationship would actually be in my best interest. This is because labeling dependency as love may constitute dishonesty toward the other person.

On the other hand, there may be concerns that if I consistently fear or avoid these somewhat confusing situations in encounters and relationships, similar patterns might simply repeat themselves in future relationships. Thus, one remains in an ambiguous state, neither ending the relationship nor fully continuing it. This is because leaving the relationship could bring freedom and new opportunities to both oneself and the other person, but it could also cause deep trauma and resentment between both parties. What, indeed, would truly be the wise course of action?

On the surface, the choices appear simple: either maintain the relationship or leave it, achieving unity in decision. However, regardless of which path one chooses, what matters more is the state of one's inner self. That is, once you recognize such a dependency structure and no longer form your relationship with that person based on dependency, that alone is already sufficient. Whether to continue the relationship or not, whether to leave the other person or stay, is rather a secondary issue.

While wanting to resolve a dependent relationship, one might initially only consider 'leaving,' yet simultaneously feel that this constitutes 'avoidance.' There is also concern that ending the relationship will leave trauma and resentment behind. We often deliberate whether ending a relationship is the right course of action, but this dilemma stems from placing greater importance on 'external behaviors' rather than our 'inner feelings.' What truly matters, however, is the state of our inner self.

Our internal emotional state is indeed influenced by our external behaviors. In some cases, physically removing oneself from a situation can help clarify the complex psychological landscape of our inner self. However, altering external behaviors without addressing and resolving our inner feelings often proves to be merely a temporary solution. If we consider leaving as the only solution when a relationship faces crisis or difficulty, we may find ourselves repeatedly unable to respond properly and fleeing again whenever similar situations arise in the future. Of course, there are times when one should leave, and times when one should part ways, but it is entirely possible to overcome crises or difficulties together and subsequently share a deeper love and relationship.

When there are problems in a relationship, regardless of whether we decide to end it or not, we must first clearly establish the goals of the relationship in our minds.

The goal is 'horizontal love' rather than 'vertical dependency.'

In relationships, 'dependency' is never one-sided. In most cases, both parties maintain dependent relationships for their own benefit. The dependent party primarily benefits from psychological dependency and the ability to shift life responsibilities, while the one being depended upon gains validation of their existence and enhanced self-esteem. In other words, if true love means 'willingly giving ourselves to each other for mutual flourishing,' dependency represents 'a mechanism of using another person for one's own well-being.' The longer the relationship continues, rather than benefiting each other, it becomes a structure where both sides are sacrificed and suffer. Sometimes, even if a relationship appears glamorous and impressive on the outside, in reality, each person's inner self moves in the opposite direction. And when it finally reaches catastrophe, it ends tragically.

This is because we humans are not beings who are meant to unilaterally depend on someone or be depended upon by others. We are beings who share love equally, horizontally, and comfortably, not beings who live in vertical relationships where one side becomes higher or lower than the other with all that entails. Such relationships are merely distortions.

First, within myself, let's attempt mature mutual sharing rather than continuing patterns of dependency. Whether I depend on others or others depend on me, the emergence of a 'dependency problem' indicates that I have not yet developed the capacity to stand independently as a healthy, mature individual. Therefore, this issue must be addressed. Externally, whether to leave or stay, whether to end a relationship or not, is secondary.

Since this is neither an obligation nor a compulsion, there is no need to feel burdened. If it doesn't work, there's no need to force it. Consider it an experimental practice. By doing so, I first cultivate within my inner self the power to engage in 'love or equal mutual sharing' rather than continuing the 'dependency mechanism' that has dominated until now. This comes from recognizing that the other person is the same kind of existence as myself—vulnerable when vulnerable, strong when strong. It means meeting each other while clearly perceiving that both of us are 'beings as we truly are'—simultaneously nothing and everything at once. At first, it may feel unfamiliar and challenging, but if you persevere with patience, even when periodic crises arise, the relationship will gradually transform into a more mature one. This is training for both relationships and life itself.

Through my own efforts, I have largely freed myself from dependent relationships, but there may be cases where the inertia of dependency still remains within the other person. The other person might reject my change, respond with anger, or attempt to sever the relationship. This is entirely possible. In essence, that represents the extent of their limitations.

In this situation, there are two choices. One is to have patience and continue striving for change to occur in both myself and him simultaneously. Of course, this doesn't mean forcing or compelling anything. There's no need to continue while suffering. All these efforts are ultimately for my own happiness. Of course, this includes wishing for the other person's happiness as well. Therefore, one can continue to be patient and make efforts. The second option is to end the relationship. This becomes necessary if the other person ultimately cannot participate in my efforts to transform vertical dependency into horizontal love. Of course, even in this case, there is no need to forcibly or reluctantly end the relationship. It is preferable to allow things to flow naturally.

Even after resolving the relationship in this manner, one may remain concerned about the possibility of similar situations recurring in the future, the potential for mutual trauma, and consequently question whether one is capable of cultivating genuine love. However, if one clearly discerns the fundamental difference between dependency and love, and achieves a degree of resolution within one's inner self, these concerns will naturally dissipate, eliminating the need for excessive worry.

At times, there are practical situations where one must terminate a relationship promptly. These are circumstances where one cannot afford the luxury of waiting for inner resolution. In such cases, there is already no justification for forcibly maintaining the relationship. Therefore, one should actively choose to end it. This requires taking decisive action. Afterward, one can continue to internally reflect upon oneself and the situation. Since reflection need not occur exclusively 'within the relationship.'

Through this process, gaining insight about the relationship will enable one to respond with greater wisdom when similar patterns emerge in the future. It is about building upon previous failures and experiences to further perfect subsequent relationships.

With horizontal love rather than vertical dependency.

◆ ◆ ◆

Summary

True love and dependency are different. Vertical dependency creates tension, while horizontal love provides comfort and freedom. What matters in relationships is the internal state rather than external behavior. Recognizing and escaping the dependency structure is essential, while maintaining or leaving the relationship remains a secondary concern. The goal should be 'horizontal love,' which means 'willingly giving oneself for the happiness of the other person.' We must strive to move beyond dependent relationships toward mature mutual sharing, which may sometimes be difficult and time-consuming but ultimately leads to healthier relationships.

5.6 You Don't Need to Be an Emotional Dumping Ground to Show Empathy

: Empathy Without Sacrifice - Feeling Others' Emotions Without Losing Yourself

- "I think I'm going to die young"

Occasionally, I engage in phone conversations with individuals seeking assistance. Several years ago, I received a call from a woman in her late fifties. She described how she and her husband constantly clashed over trivial matters, and how their attempts at conversation quickly deteriorated into arguments, leading her to conclude she could no longer continue living this way. She explained that while she had tolerated these circumstances in her youth, she now found herself unable to endure them any longer. This is entirely understandable. How could anyone be expected to endure indefinitely?

Just the other day, during an argument, I impulsively mentioned 'divorce,' and my husband suddenly became serious, asking me to endure for just one more year until our child graduates from college. He said after that year, he would disappear from my life. She told me her heart sank upon hearing her husband's words. Her husband suffers from chronic conditions, including myocardial infarction, and has frequently mentioned that he expects to die prematurely.

Of course, she acknowledged that she fully understands separating now would not benefit either of them. However, due to continuous arguments and conflicts, the stress between them had reached its peak. No matter how they tried to resolve it, nothing seemed to work. She mentioned that her husband's birthday was the next day, but she felt so upset that she didn't even want to prepare the traditional birthday seaweed soup for him. Nevertheless, she strongly felt the need to fundamentally improve their relationship. That's why she had reached out with a phone call.

During our conversation, perhaps due to her anxiety, she asked if I could offer immediate advice. So I told her there was one principle of unity I could share. I first asked if she would be willing to try exactly what I suggested. Because knowing the method is useless if not implemented. Fortunately, she agreed to try.

First, I asked how she responds when her husband says, 'I think I'm going to die young.' She said she responds with things like, 'Don't say such unlucky things, words can become reality.' So I advised her. From now on, when your husband says that, set aside your own thoughts and feelings momentarily and first try to empathize with his emotional state. Don't try to do anything else, just feel it by thinking, 'This must be what my husband is feeling now, this must be his emotional state when he says such things...'

I instructed her to express those feelings in this way. (In such cases, empathizing with the other person's emotions is essential, but verbally expressing this understanding is equally important.)

"You're really that anxious about it, aren't you? You're also very worried about your health... I didn't fully understand your feelings before. Now I think I understand a little better....

After a moment, sobbing could be heard from the other end of the phone. She said that now she seems to understand what she had been unaware of before. And what she had done wrong. My heart also grew solemn alongside hers.

Many speak about the importance of empathy. Providing genuine empathy is not easy. There are abundant theories, but empathy in reality remains challenging. Nevertheless, properly empathizing at crucial moments is immensely valuable to us.

Empathy is quite simple. It's simple, yet people struggle because they don't truly understand it.

If you wish to empathize effectively and authentically with someone you care about, here is a method. Let's momentarily set aside the numerous theories, perspectives, and advice about empathy that we've encountered thus far. If you truly want to practice genuine empathy, begin with this approach.

Don't simply validate that the other person is right, agree with them, abandon your own feelings, or dismiss your experience while accommodating their feelings, mood, or emotions.

Simply experience what they are feeling alongside them. When you share in their feelings this way, their heart will naturally begin to heal as well.

It's not just easy in theory, but actually easy in practice. If it feels difficult, let's consider the following explanation a bit further. (What if it still doesn't work? That's alright. It's perfectly acceptable if you struggle with empathy. You can live well regardless. This kind of light-hearted mindset is beneficial.)

This is not merely a theory, but rather the fundamental principle of how our minds naturally function. Then what about all those existing explanations of empathy? They were all essentially describing this same principle. Therefore, all those explanations are valid. However, it became somewhat complicated because I attempted to be too comprehensive or provide excessive detail. Additionally, most explanations yield meaningful results when practiced faithfully and consistently. Therefore, it is beneficial to read and implement any theory or explanation regarding empathy.

'Simply feeling what another person is feeling' becomes natural once you experience its effectiveness a few times—you'll find yourself doing it instinctively. This natural and simple principle of feeling together with others and allowing the mind to unwind. Even if you don't succeed at first, don't be discouraged; simply continue to practice with persistence. This is an inherent human capacity that we all possess, though it may have become somewhat dulled over time.

When you practice 'empathic resonance,' something remarkable accompanies it. It is precisely the effect of 'the other person's emotional barriers dissolving.' This phenomenon occurs naturally when empathic resonance is properly achieved, so there's no need to consciously focus on it. Rather than viewing it as an obligation or objective, it emerges organically as a natural consequence. Furthermore, when the other person's heart becomes unburdened, my own heart finds relief as well. Once you experience this, you will become increasingly drawn to the transformative power of this approach.

- Let's not mistake non-empathy for genuine empathy

'Feeling what the other person is feeling' should be taken quite literally. So simply try it first. However, if you're not yet sufficiently familiar with this concept, some explanation might be helpful, so let's explore it in greater depth.

First, why do we find empathy so difficult?

In short, it is because we misunderstand what empathy truly is. We believe we must tell others they are right, agree with them unconditionally, and abandon or ignore our own feelings to fully accept theirs.

This is not the case. There is no need for that!

Let me be clear: that is not empathy. That's precisely why it feels difficult and burdensome. These are, in fact, genuinely difficult and challenging things to do. We clearly have our own thoughts, feelings, opinions, emotions, and sense of right and wrong, so how can we assert that only the other person's perspective is correct? Indeed, we should not do this. If we do so, even if the other person survives, I perish instead. When I perish, the relationship dies as well. That is not what empathy truly is. Empathy is about preserving both the other person and myself.

Therefore, from now on, do not claim to be empathetic while forcibly or reluctantly agreeing that the other person is right, correct, or worthy of agreement. Do not unconditionally accept their emotions, ignore your own feelings, or try to force yourself to understand the other person. Such behavior is not only a betrayal of myself, but the other person's satisfaction is also momentary and does not endure. The other person quickly senses my true inner feelings. Even if I don't clearly perceive it in the moment, something unsettling remains in my mind. This creates a negative influence—both on myself and on the other person.

- Simply share in what the other person is experiencing

Now, we have entered the genuine phase.
So you're saying I should feel what the other person is feeling?
But how?
As I mentioned before, maintain your own feelings, thoughts, judgments, and understanding as they are. There is no need to change or eliminate them. While retaining all of these aspects of yourself, simultaneously experience what the other person is feeling. You can express this through words or actions later, but for now, let's simply focus on the feeling itself. It's straightforward and carries no burden.

You can simply accept the feelings that arise within you, or alternatively, you can inquire directly with the other person. "How are you feeling right now?" Simply asking this question can create a tremendous difference. Previously, I often had no understanding of the other person's emotional state, or my assumptions were incorrect. However, by asking and directly hearing about their feelings, I gain insight effortlessly. No complex or difficult process is required. One simply needs to ask. If you can sense their feelings to some degree without asking, then simply focus on experiencing that sensation fully.

Occasionally, even this approach may not be effective. This happens when I struggle to connect emotionally, or when the other person fails to respond adequately to my inquiries.

In such instances, we should employ our imagination. Try to imagine the emotions I would experience if I were in the other person's position—in that situation where I might feel wronged, angry, sad, or depressed. 'If I were in that position, how would I feel right now?' I can recall emotions from similar situations I've experienced in the past. Then, I simply allow myself to feel those same emotions. It is recognizing that the other person is likely experiencing similar feelings, emotions, and moods as we are in this moment.

This power of imagination is an inherent ability that all humans naturally possess. When watching dramas, movies, or reading novels, we feel the emotions of the protagonist or characters precisely because of this ability. So it would be untrue to claim we cannot do this. We simply haven't focused on developing it yet. For people we cherish, are close to, or love, 'feeling together with them' happens naturally, even when we're instructed not to do so.

Still not working well? Of course, that can happen. Everything requires some degree of concentration and repetition. If you carefully follow the steps mentioned earlier, you'll eventually begin to sense, 'This is how you must be feeling right now.' The emotions we experience as humans are remarkably similar to one another.

However, there is an important point of caution here. This is more of a 'feeling' rather than a conjecture or speculation. It resembles the natural way we sense the emotions and feelings of a protagonist in a film. If you rely on conjecture or assumptions, you may fail to experience genuine feelings. Occasionally, people lament, 'Why do I always misinterpret situations despite my efforts to empathize?' This occurs because they hastily make intellectual assumptions rather than truly experiencing the feelings. They're attempting to guess the other person's mood, emotions, and feelings.

It naturally fails when approached through intellectual reasoning alone. While guesses or assumptions may intervene, even if some assumptions are made, the key is to focus on 'feeling the feelings.' This is the most essential technique. Even if there are initially differences between your perception and the other person's actual feelings, continued practice will naturally enhance your sensitivity over time. Therefore, rather than excessive concern, persistence is the key to improvement.

Some individuals pursue empathy training through reading books, attending programs, and studying communication techniques. Initially, they may experience some success, only to soon encounter significant obstacles. While theoretical frameworks suggest progress should occur, reality often presents a different outcome. Even when I empathize, I don't feel particularly good about it, and the other person either shows no special reaction or seems to respond slightly at first before quickly becoming indifferent.

A husband reportedly learned an 'empathy technique' as a unifying approach through his company's training program. The technique was to 'repeat what the other person says.' This is commonly called 'backtracking,' or sometimes mimicking, providing verbal affirmations, or the technique of active agreement.

So when he applied it to conversations with his wife at home, wow, it really seemed to work. Even though I merely echo my wife's words back to her, she appears to feel understood and speaks with enthusiasm.

As I continue employing this method, I notice my wife's responsiveness gradually diminishing. Eventually, one day my wife confronts her attentive husband with: "Just with words?"

Though a simple example, this is drawn from actual experience. So, I followed the technique correctly—what could be the problem?

The primary issue is 'not genuinely feeling the other person's current emotions within my own heart.' I have no particular enthusiasm, and neither does the other person. We are merely applying techniques mechanically. Of course, this is far more admirable, useful, and commendable than doing nothing at all. Therefore, if possible, let us endeavor to try our best.

The problem is this. When we employ empathy techniques halfheartedly or strategically, we assume the other person will neither recognize nor sense our insincerity. However, our unconscious is surprisingly sensitive and wise. It comprehends everything to a certain degree. It's about whether your heart is truly experiencing my heart's emotions in unison with mine.

In such moments, our most powerful strategy is what we call 'co-feeling'—feeling together with them.

It's simply about sharing in the emotion or mood that they appear to be experiencing. Initially, you may be uncertain whether what you're sensing is accurate. The feeling might be subtle. At first, it might merely be your own projection. Your initial intuition might not align with their actual experience. But if you persist steadily without giving up, you'll begin to sense changes—as though you can feel the magnetic field shifting when the distant magnet moves, or perceive the vibrations of a remote oscillator. This phenomenon could be described as 'resonance(共鳴)'. We all possess this capability. It is innate to every human being.

Rather than approaching this as an obligation, responsibility, or empathy exercise, engage with it playfully—like a 'feeling-together game'—without any pressure. Humans are inherently born with the ability to sense each other's hearts (emotions), and we can practice this by acknowledging that we are constantly perceiving these feelings. Approach this not with excessive seriousness or heaviness, but rather as an enjoyable, lighthearted exercise.

The reason we fail to properly sense emotions, despite possessing empathic capabilities, is simply because we have not been attentive to or focused on what we are already feeling. Now, instead of feeling obligated to agree with his thoughts, feelings, opinions, or unconditionally accommodate his mood, let us simply pay more attention to his emotions as we perceive them. Then you can reconnect with what you were originally feeling.

At some point (or perhaps immediately at the beginning), there will come a moment when you properly recognize, 'Ah, this is the sensation, this is the mood, this is the emotion!' Even if that doesn't happen, it's perfectly fine. Simply continuing to acknowledge these feelings together is sufficient. This practice alone produces invisible positive effects. However, when the moment arrives that you truly connect with the feeling, you will experience a profound sense of revelation. After that point, it becomes much easier and more natural. And even without being instructed to do so, you may naturally desire to sense the other person's feelings.

I may be making an effort to empathize with the other person in my own way, yet they might still express dissatisfaction or complain that I don't understand them. Observing such reactions, you might feel disappointed or lose motivation, perceiving that your efforts go unappreciated.

Let us reconsider this perspective. Was not the original purpose of 'empathizing together' something beyond seeking the other person's understanding or gratitude? As a result, the other person may feel grateful, but initially, the purpose and outcome is simply for me to experience these feelings, regardless of other considerations. When this mindset is firmly established, you can continue to connect with the other person without being swayed by their reactions. That is the goal.

When we properly connect and feel together in this way, the remarkable phenomenon that follows is the 'unburdening of the heart.'

When I engage authentically with my feelings, the other person's emotional defenses also tend to naturally dissolve. This is truly a profound experience. Sometimes we can even intuit that this might be the case. 'If I express this now, that person's heart will be unburdened,' we think to ourselves. This is a phenomenon that occurs when invisible empathy genuinely manifests between two people. Though I cannot explain it scientifically, this phenomenon undeniably occurs in reality. I'm referring to the phenomenon where when I sincerely attune to another's mood, emotions, and feelings, their heart naturally opens and finds relief.

There is no need to make this your objective. There may be times when you think, 'I believe I'm responding appropriately, so why isn't that person's heart opening up?' In such moments, you can simply think with patience, 'Perhaps this needs more time to mature.' If you continue 'feeling together' as you originally intended, regardless of outcomes, you will experience situations of conflict, tension, and disagreement gradually resolving themselves. 'Feeling together' is both the goal and the outcome in itself; therefore, any attempt to artificially manipulate something through this process becomes yet another obstacle. Therefore, let us proceed wisely, with a light and flexible mindset.

- Whenever possible, directly express what I am feeling

It is beneficial to sense the other person's mood and emotions, but should I merely perceive them without response?

No. While perception is certainly most important, expressing it through words or actions amplifies the effect. Therefore, effective expression is also essential.

For instance, one might speak while simultaneously connecting with the other person's feelings, mood, and emotional state.

"Yes. You must be feeling ~ right now."
"Are you feeling ~ right now?"
"I'm really sorry. You must be feeling ~, and I didn't realize it."
"Now I understand that you're feeling ~."

If you can demonstrate it through actions, that would be beneficial as well. Empathetic facial expressions, speech patterns, tone of voice, phrasing, and gestures are also effective. Rather than being a specialized technique, simply allow your natural feelings to emerge authentically.

After expressing my feelings, the other person might respond with something like, 'I'm not actually feeling that way right now.' Then, one should simply acknowledge that their capacity for empathic attunement is still developing. Or perhaps the other person may not be ready to respond to your empathy yet. There is no need to feel disappointed or discouraged by such a reaction. Simply continue to develop your capacity to sense and connect with others' emotions. Be vigilant not to allow vague assumptions, inferences, or expectations to interfere. Let us practice, in the most literal sense, 'simply feeling together.' Remember that the act of empathic feeling itself is both the objective and the outcome.

Until these efforts become familiar and transform into daily habits, the journey may remain challenging, with small hurdles to overcome along the way. But it is entirely natural to need this 'process time,' and progress comes from surmounting these challenges one by one as you move forward. With each hill you overcome, you become more psychologically mature, experience more moments of happiness, and develop a richer, more fulfilling life.

◆ ◆ ◆

Summary

True empathy is simply the ability to feel another person's emotions. This is not about abandoning your own emotions or unconditionally accepting the other person's emotions. The methods of empathy are as follows:

1) Feeling the other person's emotions,

2) Employing imagination when necessary,

3) Expressing the emotions you have felt.

Empathy requires practice, and it is important to enjoy the process without becoming fixated on the results. True empathy can open the other person's heart and improve relationships. This is not a technique but a natural human capacity that can be enhanced through consistent practice.

5.7 Apology for Myself, for Others, for All

: Beyond Right and Wrong

Apologizing is difficult for everyone.
Whether I am in a superior position,
an equal position,
or an inferior position—it affects us all.

There are many reasons why apologizing is difficult.
When I feel there is no reason for me to apologize,
When apologizing will cause me to lose something,
When I think the other person should apologize instead,
When I know I should apologize but it wounds my pride,
When I believe my apology will have no effect on the other
person...

In any case
The real reason why it is difficult for us to apologize properly
is because
we do not know for whom the apology is intended.

An apology is not for myself
nor is it for the other person.
It is for both myself and the other person.

This does not mean it is for each of us 'separately.'
If it were for each separately,
it would ultimately be the same as being either for myself or for
the other person.
There would be no difference.

A genuine apology is not like that.

Those who benefit from an apology
are not the separate 'self and other'
but the newly formed unity of 'both self and other.'

When my position and your position are considered separately
Clearly determining who is more right or wrong
According to that outcome
It is not about who apologizes to whom.

Within that event, that situation, that flow
Mutually engaging and interpenetrating (相即相入)
A new wholeness of perspective emerges.

Not two separate entities
Duality within unity.
Also, a modality that is unity but with the polarity of two.

When we experience this perspective,
When we come to stand in this position,
Whoever apologizes first,
when a heartfelt, sincere apology is felt,
it emerges naturally,
and whoever receives the apology
experiences a resonant heart response.
And thus, forgiveness arises.

At that moment, it's no longer about who apologized and felt
humiliated,
or who received the apology and feels superior,

but rather how two hearts connected in unity
unravel together
and melt into one another.

A true apology,
is not for my benefit,
nor is it for your benefit,
It is not for self and other, nor for each of us individually.

A true apology,
As a new wholeness with dual polarity
It exists for 'both self and other.'

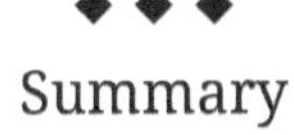

Summary

A genuine apology serves not the individual, but 'us' as a collective. While there are various reasons why apologizing is difficult, fundamentally it stems from not knowing who the true recipient of the apology is. An apology is not meant for 'me' or 'you' separately, but for the new 'we' that we create together. This involves understanding the interconnected dynamics where we influence each other, rather than merely considering individual perspectives or making judgments about right and wrong. A genuine apology creates a moment where two connected hearts unravel together and melt into unity.

5.8 Rediscovering Myself Through Another

: Beyond the Self - A Journey Through Others

I Through You, You Through Me
Completing Self-Love.
Completing Self-Existence.

Humans Are Relational Beings. Throughout life, we form and dissolve various types of relationships: friendships, romantic partnerships, marriages...

And we also have children. There are teaching and learning relationships as well.

Perhaps 'forming relationships' is one of the most mysterious phenomena in existence. This is because it represents a process through which an individual exists beyond the boundaries of the self. What is achieved through forming relationships is not merely 'the meeting of self and other' but rather 'encountering oneself through another self.' These 'selves' are no longer the same as one's previous identity.

Relationships become a method for completing self-love. They present an opportunity for wholeness.

Among various relationships, the most mysterious one is 'bringing a child into the world.' Of course, I am not suggesting that relationships with friends, lovers, or teachers and students are any less profound. All contain sufficient meaning and mystery within them. However, the act of giving birth to a child contains a more direct intensity, both physically and mentally.

Through their own baby, a parent encounters for the first time 'the self beyond self, the self outside of self' as a vivid reality. For parents, babies even become 'a self more precious than myself.'

A self more precious than myself! This seems like a mysterious, inexplicable experience that would only be possible through profound philosophy or religion.

Not only humans but all existing living beings create offspring. To explain it in the most clinical terms, it would be called the instinct for species reproduction or species preservation.

From another perspective, this could also be called 'the instinct to meet oneself through another self.' The purpose of such meeting is to complete self-love. In other words, it is also about completing one's self-existence. Perhaps rather than being conscious, it could be viewed as a predominantly unconscious or archetypal phenomenon.

The self-love of existence is not necessarily completed only through children. It can readily occur in other types of relationships as well. Furthermore, the relationship between parents and children is not always positive and beneficial. At times, it can become tragic or destructive.

What parents experience, even including these negative elements, is ultimately the overcoming of attachment to, illusion about, or ignorance of 'a self constituted solely of one's individual existence.' Perhaps this could be an even more profound and intense experience than the non-self (無我) spoken of in Buddhism—if one properly experiences and recognizes it. However, even as parents, if they become complacent about their children, prioritize their own desires, and overlook aspects that should be maintained and respected for mutual benefit, they will create difficulties for one another. In essence, effort, self-awareness, and insight are necessary.

All relationships we form contain such archetypal elements.

Therefore,

In any relationship we establish in life,

Until the connection has fulfilled its purpose and comes to an end,

Let us cherish and nurture it with our utmost dedication.

Every relationship is an opportunity.
Not exclusively for myself or exclusively for the other
Beyond myself and the other, for existence itself.
And for the fulfillment of self-love among all beings.

Summary

A relationship is a process of self-transcendence, not 'meeting others through myself' but rather 'meeting myself through others'. The parent-child relationship, in particular, is the most profound connection that allows us to directly experience 'the self beyond the self'. This can be understood not merely as an instinct for species preservation, but as 'the instinct to discover oneself through others'. All relationships provide opportunities to complete self-love and fulfill our existence. Therefore, we must cherish and nurture all relationships, not simply for individual benefit, but for the sake of existence itself and the completion of existence's self-love.

5.9 You and I: Not Two Separate Entities, But One with Dual Polarities

: Exploring the concept of unity in relationships

I have been contemplating and using the expression 'duality within unity' for some time now.

(Here, in the place of 'two', 'N' can be inserted, and this N is a real number that can extend to infinity.)

When applying this to human relationships, it can be expressed as follows:

You and I are not two separate entities, but 'Duality within unity.'

For example, lovers or spouses are not two separate entities, but a 'new wholeness with a polarity of two.' When there are Mother, father, and children in a Family, they are not several separate entities, but a 'new wholeness with multiple polarities.' When there is a group where multiple people are connected, they are not separate individuals but 'a new wholeness with corresponding polarity.'

They are two yet one, and one yet two. They are neither completely separated entities nor a homogenized unity. They are 'a new wholeness with multiple polarities.' This applies to lovers, couples, families, and groups.

Now the ultimate goal of that relationship or group becomes not the happiness of the individual 'self' but the happiness of the 'new wholeness.'

If we ignore this point and stubbornly maintain our individual positions, perspectives, and pursuit of happiness while mistakenly believing we are completely separate entities, that new wholeness will only become painful. This explains why many lovers, couples, and families desire happiness, yet ultimately none achieve it. It is because they fail to pursue the happiness of the 'new wholeness' that undeniably exists. They consider only the separate polarities.

Conversely, problems also arise when considering only the whole without regard for the position or happiness of each polarity (individual). The whole consists of various polarities, yet it presents itself as if polarity does not exist. It becomes a 'unity that disregards polarity.' Polarity undeniably continues to exist. Therefore, it must be acknowledged and considered.

Neither individualism nor collectivism can ever be the complete answer.

We must approach from the perspective of a 'new wholeness with N polarities.'

If problems between lovers, couples, family members, or group constituents are not resolving well, it becomes necessary to flexibly, actively, and wisely select methods and solutions that—depending on the situation and needs—sometimes consider polarity, sometimes unity, and sometimes both aspects simultaneously.

Are you struggling or feeling dissatisfied because your partner, spouse, child, or parents are not behaving as you wish? If so, let us examine whether you might be stubbornly adhering to only your own perspective as a polarity, or to the perspective of another person as a polarity. Consider whether you or the other person might be centering actions solely around one polarity. We should seek what serves the 'new wholeness' that encompasses all polarities. We should focus on what the original goal truly is.

In many cases, we fail to abandon our 'position of polarity,' persistently insisting on what is satisfying and happy solely from our individual perspective. Now, rather than maintaining such a perspective, even if 'this polarity' that constitutes our individual self is not satisfied, we should temporarily set aside our stubbornness and consider 'what would make the whole unity happy?' This involves taking other polarities into account.

New solutions and methods that were previously invisible will begin to appear and emerge. When the unified whole achieves happiness, the self and other as polarities within it also experience happiness together. Similarly, when all polarities equally share in happiness, the unified whole becomes happy. We should approach each situation appropriately.

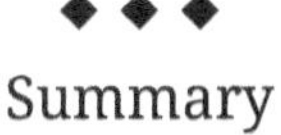

Summary

In human relationships, 'self' and 'other' are not separate existences but can be viewed as 'one entity with dual polarity'. This principle applies to all relationships including romantic partners, couples, family, and groups. The ultimate goal of such relationships is not individual happiness but the happiness of the 'new wholeness'. Rather than pursuing complete separation or homogenization, one must consider the positions of each polarity and the whole in a balanced manner. To solve problems, wisdom and flexibility are needed to consider the perspectives of polarity, the whole, or both simultaneously, depending on the situation. When the whole becomes happy, each polarity also becomes happy, and when each polarity is equally happy, the whole becomes happy as well.

5.10 Two Truths (N Truths - N Ranges from 0 to Infinity)

From 'My Truth' to 'Our Truths' - Embracing Multiple Realities

Personal conflicts or concerns such as self-hatred

Or those occurring in relationships between two or more individuals

In various conflicts

What everyone considers important is

'What is correct' or

'Who is right.'

We all

Whether it concerns an individual matter or involves multiple parties

Eventually seek 'one correct unity, one true unity'

Must find and establish it

For that situation to be resolved

Because we believe this to be necessary.

Precisely,

It is the belief in 'a single truth.'

/

However,

Due to certain educational influences and indoctrinations

Besides unconscious beliefs that were formed without my awareness

there is no evidence to support

'a unity of truth.'

Of course, depending on the situation,
whose words are closer to the facts or
closer to common sense and universality
there are certainly times when we must examine precisely.
In such cases,
we must carefully consider and reach an accurate, appropriate
conclusion.
This is self-evident.

However,
cases where we need to strictly distinguish right from wrong in
daily life
are not that numerous.
Most of the time, regardless of who is right or wrong,
it doesn't make much difference in life.

Even in such moments, we
persistently try to determine who is right and wrong.
We want recognition that I, our side, is right, correct, and accurate.
We seek acknowledgment.

'I am the truth. That one truth is mine!'
It's a kind of desire for validation.

This is largely unconscious and
an automatic response.
The notion that 'there is only one truth'
has not been proven or
confirmed by anyone.

We simply feel that way, consider it
and believe it.

When we become aware of this,
many things change.

A more accurate and useful expression is
'There are N truths.'

The 'single truth' that everyone
still prefers is certainly possible,
as are the 'two truths' between you and me.
And even 'N truths' among all of us.
'Wouldn't that create too much confusion?'
one might worry.
Correct. That can be the case.

So there is something of utmost importance.
This also is not a forced directive or the only correct answer.
That is, even the concept of 'N truths' is not the only truth.

The concept of 'N truths' within this phrase
is not a rule created for complacency
but finds its value solely in how well it is applied.
If this approach proves more useful and effective
then willingly embrace it.

We are not slaves to truth
but rather its masters.

Therefore, when 'a single truth' is needed

Let's also willingly embrace this approach.
However, while doing so, let's always remain open to
the possibility of two truths, or even multiple truths.

So, from now on,
if the belief in, insistence upon, and imposition of 'a single truth'
causes suffering to self, other, and our collective well-being,
let's not unnecessarily cling to that singular perspective.
Let's acknowledge 'my truth' while also honoring 'your truth.'
And if necessary, let's also consider
many other 'collective truths' together.

Thus, problems that remained unsolvable when insisting on 'a
single truth'
'Two truths'
That is, when we can simultaneously perceive both the truth of
self and other
That is precisely what constitutes genuine wisdom.
Quite a number of conflicts, clashes, and problems
Can be resolved in this manner.

The real goal is the happiness of self and other, and ultimately us
collectively
Not some abstract notion of 'truth'.

/

Finally, a small joke.

Perhaps our feeling, perception, and belief
That 'truth is unity'

Might stem from the fact that the sun we observe is singular.

Humanity has observed this single sun since ancient times
We see it continuously from birth, and we all keep observing it together
Perhaps this has created an instinctive feeling that 'truth must also be singular!'
This might be how such a notion developed.

If the sun were two or more
on some planet where we were born,
we might now believe that truth follows the same pattern
Who can say for certain?

Of course, this is merely a jest.

But the reason I'm offering this whimsical thought is
because this illustrates how we've come to believe that 'truth is unity'
That feeling and belief
Because it can be viewed very lightly.

Also, it is
Because it is actually very light in nature.
(Except when circumstances require us to treat it with gravity)

◆ ◆ ◆

Summary

We often believe that a single truth exists, but this is merely an unconscious belief system instilled by education and society. In most everyday situations, strictly distinguishing between right and wrong is unnecessary. 'Truth exists in N forms' is a concept that can be more useful and accurate. This encompasses a single truth, two truths (yours and mine), and our collective N number of truths. This approach should be utilized as a tool rather than a rigid rule, and should be applied flexibly according to the circumstances. The true objective is not truth itself, but rather the happiness of myself, you, and us collectively. This perspective can help resolve numerous conflicts and interpersonal tensions.

Afterword | Don't Strive to Be Happy. Create 'Happiness Itself'

Every human being desires happiness. In most cases, people believe that to achieve happiness, certain conditions must be fulfilled. These constitute what we might call the prerequisites for happiness. However, strictly speaking, 'happiness is also a feeling, not content.'

Readers of this book will now understand that this does not mean 'content is not important at all' or 'content is unnecessary.' Let us develop and cultivate the content we desire in the wisest and most meaningful way. There is nothing we cannot do and nothing we should not do. To achieve this, let us actively transform not only ourselves as individuals but society as a whole.

Let us recognize that happiness is not determined solely by or because of its content. Ultimately, all of that content is merely used to create 'feelings of happiness.' The essence lies not in the content but in the feeling itself. The content, while necessary, is actually secondary.

We are too fixated on content—that is, on conditions. While it's beneficial to use these as appropriate means toward happiness, we need not believe that happiness is impossible without fulfilling specific conditions. The same applies to the belief that happiness is only attainable when possessing certain attributes recognized by others, society, and culture. It means sacrificing our original goal of happiness and the feeling of happiness for the sake of conditions that are merely secondary. Both individuals and society are equally guilty of this. The priorities have become completely reversed. The subject and object have been inverted.

Perhaps this is why our society and its individuals experience more unnecessary suffering compared to other countries or societies. Both individuals and society must undergo transformation. Individuals must transform themselves to properly cultivate their own happiness, while society must simultaneously evolve alongside them. This is our collective duty and responsibility, as well as our inherent right.

When we prioritize only 'content' in our pursuit of happiness, both individuals and societies inevitably chase misguided objectives. These include outdated approaches from the past, conforming to others' and society's expectations rather than our own desires, exploiting others for individual or collective gain, maintaining a narrow perspective that serves only oneself rather than the whole, and supporting biased laws, systems, politics, and economic structures that benefit only certain groups.

All of these represent potential side effects that emerge when we excessively pursue fossilized 'content' rather than authentic happiness and its genuine experience. And currently, our society is failing. Why is that? Content cannot be a condition for happiness. For you and me to be truly happy and to experience genuine feelings of happiness, we must no longer be manipulated by content but rather learn to utilize it. We must continuously seek out and transform the content that is truly essential. If something is useful, we should continue to employ it; however, if it no longer serves us and instead inflicts unnecessary suffering upon individuals and society, we must be courageous enough to release it—both on personal and societal levels.

While this book does not focus primarily on happiness, resolving the issues of self-hatred, projection, identity, trauma, and relationships discussed within will increasingly bring happiness as a natural result. This is not to say that the book itself creates this outcome, but rather that successfully overcoming life challenges in these five areas leads to such results.

Some readers may find the perspectives, value systems, and concepts presented in this book deeply engaging and familiar, while others might experience them as somewhat unfamiliar or distant. Some may find this contrary to their usual way of thinking. Additionally, even for a single individual, certain content in the book may resonate deeply while other parts may feel distant. This is perfectly acceptable. What matters is that if there is even one element of this book's content that can bring greater happiness to you and your life, you should diligently practice it until it becomes your own. Not because someone instructed you to do so. You desire this for yourself and act accordingly. We all possess such inner strength in our lives.

I sincerely hope that all readers of this book will find true happiness. Not through what others and society impose, but through what one actively chooses for oneself. Furthermore, beyond any external content whatsoever. Not by pursuing happiness as defined by others, but by becoming the author of one's own definition of happiness.

- End -

About The Author

MuRu

MuRu is a meditative psychoanalyst. He has been operating 'The MuRu Center' in Korea for more than 15 years. His professional domains encompass 'counseling, education, coaching, and consulting' in the fields of 'meditation, consciousness, and psychology'.

With a profound interest in human psychology and consciousness, he has thoroughly explored various Eastern and Western meditation techniques and theories, as well as psychology and neuroscience, applying these insights to psychological counseling, education, coaching, and consulting programs. Generally, meditation excels in fundamental approaches to human existence but falls short in addressing specific psychological issues. Psychology, conversely, demonstrates strength in addressing specific psychological issues but lacks depth in fundamental approaches to human existence.

Author MuRu has created and utilizes an approach called 'Meditative psychoanalysis' that harmonizes the strengths of meditation and psychology through extensive experience and research. This approach presents diagnoses and solutions by uniquely integrating modern achievements in psychology and neuroscience with traditional and fundamental wisdom and insights from meditation and other practices for the psychoanalysis of individuals and groups.

For this purpose, the author also employs his own 'Meta-cognitive methodology'. Meta-cognition can be explained as 'thoughts about thoughts, thinking that embraces and transcends ordinary cognition.' It involves approaching from a completely liberated perspective without unconditionally accepting existing thoughts, fixed ideas, and concepts. To achieve this, one avoids treating any thought as absolute, and instead recognizes thought itself as an object to be examined.

In essence, 'meta-cognition' is a methodology for becoming the master of one's thoughts rather than their slave. It enables free and creative thinking without being trapped in the prison and frame of established thought patterns. Throughout the book 'Self-Hatred', MuRu's meta-cognitive thinking method is introduced, which 'willingly embraces various positive and negative thoughts and memories while simultaneously transcending them'.

Additionally, the author's psychological analysis emphasizes the 'simultaneity of individual and collective society'. This means that any phenomenon or problem involves both elements to varying degrees, and there are no cases that are purely individual or purely societal in nature. MuRu's 'Meditative psychoanalysis' always considers both the individual and collective society as its subjects.

For approximately ten years on Korea's Brunch service, I have written nearly 500 articles across various categories including psychology, Enlightenment, everyday insights, and film reviews. (https://brunch.co.kr/@philosophus). Currently, the readership exceeds 10,000, with total views approaching 2 million.

MuRu has published two books in Korea. One is "Self-Hatred" and the other is "MuRu's Enlightenment". The full title including the subtitle is, "Self-Hatred - Why Do We Hate Ourselves? Beyond Self-Hatred, Methods to Regain Inner Peace" and "MuRu's Enlightenment - Embracing and Transcending Reason, Religion, and Spirituality, Toward an Era of Self-Awareness and Awakening". Currently, both books are being translated and published in Japanese and English, with plans for translation and publication in various countries across Europe and Asia. (Individuals or publishing houses interested in collaborating on the translation and publication of these two books can contact The MuRu Center to discuss and proceed with specific collaboration arrangements.)

Email address: philosophus@naver.com

Books By This Author

- **"Self-Hatred"**
  : Beyond Self-Hatred, How to Regain Peace of Mind

"Self-Hatred" is a book that presents profound analysis and solutions for the psychological phenomenon of self-hatred afflicting modern individuals. It is based on MuRu's decades of psychological counseling experience and employs MuRu's unique 'Meditative psychoanalysis' technique.

This book encompasses the theme of 'self-hatred' along with healing methods for various traumas, approaches to protect oneself from emotional wounds in daily life, insights into interpersonal relationships, and guidance for psychological maturity. The distinctive feature of this book is that it is written from a 'psychological perspective based on principles of Enlightenment,' encompassing and transcending general psychology.

Every person harbors some degree of self-hatred. This originates from self-boundaries and self-reflection, but the problem arises when this psychology exceeds normal levels and manifests as self-deprecation, a sense of guilt, and feelings of culpability. To overcome this, one must understand and bring into consciousness the hidden mechanisms of self-hatred. At the root of self-hatred exist self-love and a superiority complex, which, when distorted, lead to negative consequences. There is an instinctive error in identifying with a negative self-image and attempting to preserve it. We must recognize our unconditional existential value rather than defining ourselves through conditional parameters. Hatred directed toward others can also be an expression of self-hatred, which must be overcome. Past traumas and wounds should not be avoided or suppressed, but willingly embraced and transcended. In human relationships, by pursuing horizontal love rather than vertical dependency, we can cultivate a more fulfilling and abundant life.

- **"MuRu's Enlightenment"**
  : Embracing and Transcending Reason, Religion, and Spirituality, Into the Age of Self-awareness and Awakening

"MuRu's Enlightenment" is a book exploring the authentic nature of enlightenment that has persisted throughout human history and the methodologies for achieving this state. This book comprises essential teachings on 'non-dualistic enlightenment,' the fundamental wisdom common to all humanity existing on Earth. It provides a detailed and profound examination of that 'singular authentic enlightenment' that has existed throughout human history across diverse regions and epochs. Enlightenment was explained very specifically as not something strange or difficult, but rather something all people can understand, and anyone can attain if they practice properly.

The 'Enlightenment' discussed in 'MuRu's Enlightenment' is precisely the same enlightenment that Shakyamuni Buddha spoke of in Buddhism. It parallels similar forms of enlightenment that have been recorded or demonstrated throughout human history, not exclusively in Buddhism. For example, it is the same enlightenment experienced by Laozi and Zhuangzi in Taoism, and in other wisdom traditions such as Dzogchen in Tibetan Buddhism, Vedanta in Hinduism, and Zen Buddhism.

These enlightenments occurred across different eras, regions, and individuals, yet the insights they contain represent the same 'shared human heritage, universal human phenomenon.' Throughout all eras and regions, individuals who have attained the same 'awakening (self-awareness)' have emerged, and their teachings have propagated, contributing to the maturation of human consciousness across all domains of civilization.

The term 'MuRu (無漏)' in the title of this book serves as both the author's name and a reference to the Buddhist concept of 'MuRu(無漏)' or impermanence. 'Muru' is the Korean pronunciation of the Chinese characters 無漏. In muru (無漏), 無 means 'nothing mu', and 漏 means 'to leak ru'. Muru (無漏), directly translated, means 'nothing more to leak,' but in Buddhism it refers to 'freedom from afflictions' or 'the absence of afflictions.' It is a term that refers to 'the state of Enlightenment where one has transcended all afflictions.' It signifies that there are no more afflictions flowing or leaking out from within. The opposing term is 'yuru (有漏)'. The meaning of yuru is 'being bound by afflictions.' This means that human afflictions and suffering continue to emerge and manifest themselves. The relationship between permanence and impermanence is similar to the correspondence between yu-wi (有爲) and mu-wi (無爲), between having-self (有我) and no-self (無我). 'MuRu's Enlightenment' does not refer to enlightenment transmitted through text and theory, or enlightenment that has become academically formalized or reduced to schematic illusions, but rather 'complete, authentic enlightenment where human suffering and anguish no longer exist.'

The key points that should be noted regarding enlightenment are as follows: In the future, where development will accelerate even more rapidly due to AI (Artificial Intelligence), 'Enlightenment' will become a crucial subject for both individuals and collectives. Particularly when AGI (Artificial General Intelligence) emerges, the possibility of humanity transcending labor and capitalism increases significantly. At that juncture, 'enlightened cognition and insight' will become more essential than ever before for the development and continuity of human collective civilization. The more widely enlightened insight spreads, the more human civilization will progress; however, without it, only complexity and scale will increase while humanity's fundamental suffering and limitations will persist or intensify.